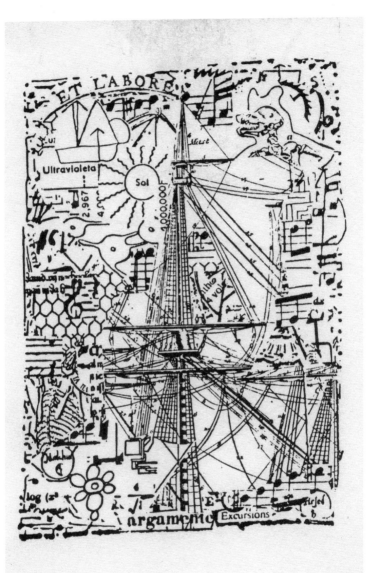

ULTRAVIOLETA

Laura Moriarty

a t e l o s

2 4

ISBN 1-891190-24-5
First edition, second printing

Cover image and frontispiece: Alan Halsey, "Sonata for the
Ancient Mariner." Used with permission of the artist.

"Targets" appeared in Roxi Hamilton's journal *viz* and
"Maryolatry" appeared in *Paraspheres*, edited by Rusty Morrison
and Ken Keegan. Thanks to the editors.

Ŧ Atelos

A Project of Hip's Road
Editors: Lyn Hejinian and Travis Ortiz
Design: Lyn Hejinian
Cover Design: Ree Katrak/Great Bay Graphics

ULTRAVIOLETA

Table of Contents

"In the black and white target language the film is called grainy; the wingless craft is seen entering the sentence a second before impact."

Alan Halsey, "Alien Proforma," *Wittgenstein's Devil*

Soon the world

"Soon the world, a series of globes."

Stella writes the world as she flees from it. She is used to traveling by her thoughts which, changeable and transparent as the clothing she wears, flow from her in palpable waves. There is a velocity to Stella's stillness as she sits writing, allowing herself to be conveyed in this metal ship. She was a child the last time she traveled on the lunar shuttle. "Earth," she thinks absently, without nostalgia. "Terra," she writes in the thick paper mechanism she calls her notebook. "Terrible," she continues.

A shadow shaped like a man falls over Stella as she works. She ignores it, continuing to make notes, as if her thinking were keeping her afloat, as if her thoughts could save her. As always, Stella attempts to define herself away, to narrate her escape from the monsters she perceives in the universe and from the ones in this place, this plane, beside her.

"Out of town and out of the world," she notes. "Earth is like the moon, the moon like Mars, honeycombed with holes, pocked with domes, invaded by light and thought. Old Mars. The new moon. Just enough time for cigarettes and tea. Everything is tea."

She takes a medicinal drag from her cigarette, feels the edge of the drug and continues to make notes.

"The new caffeine. The one good thing about the old world. Being gone. The last ride of the next century. Something is always ending and this is ending now. This being in the world. This time. I am gone from it. Each time the light ends in me I am more present and more gone."

Stella looks up at the back of a head. It is the source of the shadow that continues to fall over her. It comes between her and the moon. She knows what will happen next but goes on as if she doesn't know.

"What is left is yellow like cream. There is light and yet there is night in the objects, making them heavy. Making us heavy. In us it is night. We take off into the night. We keep the books. *History of Space Travel. Universal Reception.* We screen them."

Stella rereads the titles she has transcribed. She scrolls through the thick paper mechanism, looking though the infinite material available from the library. As anyone, Stella reads to travel but, unlike most readers, Stella travels well. Manuals, histories, books of poetry are like fuel to her, like bulletins from the gone worlds. The many worlds.

"How far can you go with your mind?" she thinks. She closes her eyes. "The I. How far can they go with it? How far can I go?"

Listening to the mind in her heart, to the inner I, the radio inside, Stella looks out. The familiar puzzle of the world articulates into recognizable landmasses and then fades, falling away, framed by the window. She looks into her notebook, searching for something to go on. She enters the names of a few writers she has found most useful to produce the kind of thinking essential to thought travel. Entering Eddie Zed produces nothing new, causing Stella to wonder if he is dead, as he never stops writing.

She enters Nahid Jones, a new name she has heard. A poem appears in the form of a frame.

Cloud cover lover bursts upon counting

Down	Vast
Kept	Stratus
Status	To verify
On stream	Bite
Body of	Work
World	Is won
War	For
Reign	Relegated to
Martians	Once

Thinking themselves for words matter
Matted with points that light upon

"A simple form," she notes, "obvious but useful, accurate. Everything is framed. Nothing is left but cloud cover," she writes as she reads, paraphrasing. "I can feel the radio in it. The radio is like rain. It is here and now. There is land below and then it is lost. Lost and gone. Out of mind, out of sight. Flying out of night into night."

She pulls down the shade of her porthole. An infomoon projects itself onto the cabin wall. She wills herself into channel scan mode. She senses the shadow again.

"How do we guard our hearts against getting caught up in the world around us?" she thinks or is it radio?

"Pale light of stars from across the aisle," she writes. Stella finds it disorienting to travel in metal rather than in mental space.

Strange not to be enveloped in a paper ship and to have no effect on one's movement.

"How can this be called being awake?" she thinks. She has the impression they will crush the moon with this metal ship instead of landing on it lightly, thoughtfully.

"Grace that saves is a gift of righteousness that purifies." The radio continues to play in Stella's head. The shadow grows darker.

Stella smokes her tea and considers the tea in her cup. She is breathless with the caffeine, though they say it helps you breathe. Stella breathes. She considers the odds of being saved. She thinks of her destination but finds she can't think of it. She thinks of grace, of Wyatt. She writes as if to save herself.

"Dear Thomas. Dear Wyatt. Renaissance guy, Gentle Master, I. I see you as a man. As Saturn, the Great Teacher. The ring thing. Mars. The war. Our time there. Jupiter like the sun."

As Stella considers the risks of her long conversation with Wyatt, the shadow grows larger and turns, rising and placing himself squarely in the light of the projected moon. He is highlighted. He is a stranger and a giant. An I — not Wyatt, but has the feel of him. His huge sight presses against her like gravity. Like Stella he seems to be a pilot. He has the insignia. He blinks formally, inwardly. Stella squints up at him as he offers an enormous hand, cool and hard.

"Pontius," he says with the monstrous charm of the I. "Pontius Pilate. I don't believe we have met."

"Stella Nemo," she replies, allowing her hand to disappear into his. "Stella," she repeats, resisting the inevitable effects of his speech.

"Enchanted," he says. Full face now like a moon, like a sun, he burns against her.

"Always happy to meet one of the boys. Been in the system long?" she asks quietly.

"Not long. People call me PP. Some call me Jack. I never know why."

"Why they call?" She plays for time.

"Why they speak at all, really. They know I can read them."

Pontius is all eyes and toothy smile. Light plays on him, illuminating what Stella knows as his *approximate organs of thought*, islands of apparent flesh which fix the attention in a way that is visceral as well as visual. She doesn't care. She looks. The first flash of heat settles over her. Something like pleasure. She wants to look away. She gets the rush. She doesn't and then she does. She sees everything, though it's not quite seeing. Time stops. More or less. As the heat breaks, she turns away to the real moon.

"Sorry," Pontius says but moves closer.

"Forget it, Jack. I am terrified and invaded but I am just a little busy right now."

"I did forget. I forgot to hold back when you…for a human…

You have an unusual capacity…"

"Yeah. Right. You guys are all alike. 'Thank you, ma'am.'"

"But I never…"

"Forget it."

Stella looks away, she focuses herself in her thinking. She writes.

"The sacred individuality of the I. You can get them there if you can take the heat. There is too much thought in their thinking. It assaults. It addles. It begs the question. Why ask? How can you survive it? And why is he a pilot? Why not? Why are they anything?"

Stella shakes herself like a dog. A bright transparency ripples through and around her. Light clings to her like water. Channel scan again. Switching away from Pontius, she considers him. The vast mask of his face hangs there. She turns herself up.

"You are a monster," she says to herself. Stella thinks in definitions. It is her only defense, that and the ability to roll with it, to go on, to travel with any thinking.

"Mordecai tore his clothes and covered himself in ashes." She hears in her head.

"Traveling alone?" Pontius pursues.

"Jesus, P. Did you just smack your lips?"

"That wasn't me. And if you are going to lay yourself out like a meal, Stella. The whole transparent…"

"As if only you can be seen through." Stella gives him a long look. "Why are you here, PP? How many pages of you are there anyway?"

"Got a gig on a boat," he replies. "Big boat. Flying some of the folks to the library. And beyond."

"But you can't get beyond the Case Barrier with a big ship, not with humans. It's been tried. There were deaths and flames." She hears the screaming in her mind, she sees the paper curl with fire. "Weren't they real flames?"

"A few hot spots," Pontius replies. "Not enough to discourage the inveterate traveler. There are regular runs now or there should be. It's a full steaming pot to The Gutenberg and this time maybe beyond, if I read my Earthlings right. That kind of travel is about letting yourself be open to each other. Let me explain."

Pontius casts himself around Stella like a net but she is too fast for him. She isolates herself in her sense of mission. She thinks of the government, always an absurd distraction. She thinks of Wyatt.

"Get to the moon," she repeats, moving mentally away from Pontius, placing herself deep within her own trajectory, Stella writhes transparent, delectable, but separate. She writes, startled, as always, startling.

"Stella," Pontius thinks, but she is beyond him now.

"Soon the world," she writes, "a series of globes. Get to the moon. Let it go. Take back off. Move through time. Thought projectile. Oneself as modem. As mode. Not something you do but something you take. Take in. It will take a while. Get all the way there. To the library satellite. The Gutenberg. Dead or alive. Single occupancy. Single occupant. Condition gone."

"Use me quiet, Wyatt," she goes on, "Pursue an untroubled existence."

No atmosphere

On the page, taking off into thought, visiting the dark where she keeps herself to herself. "I," she thinks, "Not. Not I, but Stella."

Stella rests in the *Nautilus* — her ship, her coffin or crypt — as the tiny paper ships are sometimes called. Here she makes the day and the diary. She makes space by traveling with and through her thinking.

"Naturally only those who can think can travel by thought," Stella thinks, gaining speed. "The limit turns out to be absolute and makes for a lot of empty space. It is a crowded universe but only on the ground. Here you are alone in the dark."

Instead of clinging to the idea of making the next stanza or the next pot, as a novice would, Stella opens out into possibility. She thinks forward, gears down, becomes oblivious, is unable to have another thought and then does. She goes on. She thinks. She reads. Sees.

"To read is to think," she thinks. "To sing is to read. And then there is radio." Stella receives, thinking and traveling singlemindedly. She writes in the diary. She lands on the asteroid Eros as lightly as it is possible for a pilot to come out of thought into the real night of space.

"At rest in the *Nautilus*," Stella writes in her notebook. "Not the first one to wind up alone on Eros. Probably not the last. But how alone? Awake in this gilded ship. Safe in the paper. Black light of the Erotic dawn. Holding steady through the flight. Work as life. A minute is an arbitrary limit like a week. Unlike a month. A stanza is a distance. A pot to piss in. An hour is a long sigh. Shut up and drive."

As navigator, Stella prepares her charts. She writes to fly, thinks and writes to keep aloft. As pilot, she drives. The room moves. In her other incarnation, she becomes the crew. One of the many travelers on the interplanetary route, Stella *is* the route. She is the rendezvous. She poses the big downstream questions. She travels on them. It is her way.

"Who are they? Who am I to them? My questions, not theirs. The government," Stella considers her erstwhile employer. It is hard to think of the I, but it is impossible to think of the government. "Hello government," she comments. Stella figures they are listening but are too preoccupied to hear. It is given that they can't think, so they can't get to you as long as you are out here. It is the whole point of thought travel for some. Others believe it is all government, all the way past Mars and beyond. The fact of the wars on Mars would seem to argue for that version. "The wars, the carnage, all that," Stella considers them. "Was that the government or the I? Did anyone really die? Or was it everyone? No one knows who is alive, except the Martians. And they are stuck on Mars, or at least they believe they are. Once a Martian, they say."

Alone with her notebook, Stella turns herself down to an antique tone of handwritten intimacy. She has made a perfect shelter of space. Resting on Eros gives her a sense of perfect safety. There are no I. No evidence that man or monster has ever set foot here before. "It is a new kind of happiness," she muses, "or unhappiness, to be this alone."

Stella smokes, she notes, she dreams in Martian grammar. She uses "whom" as the relative pronoun in the accusative case. She speaks in I. She sings. Melody and then recorded melody. Informational espionage. Terror. Life on the rock. Cuts. Old radio. Very old rock. New rock. A new cut.

"Motive? Now there is a thought," she thinks in a burst of caffeinated revery.

Night drains away leaving what feels like a replica of the asteroid in her belly, of stars like suns in her eyes, but it is still night. She reviews her procedures manual as if it was a poem, whistling to herself in the language of the monsters.

"Morning edition," she thinks, turning up the radio in her mind. "It is always morning somewhere." She scans and monitors, watching, listening. "You can picture the radio," she writes, "while it pictures you. Real space. Real radio. Hidden in the clock. The clock as ship. As shift. Oneself suspended as in a locket. Locket rocket thinking through radiographic space."

"Satan will never tempt you to something you didn't like anyway," she hears.

"Suddenly faint with exhaustion," she writes. "A world without things. We have a fear of speech. We fear the whispering and the government. The record collection. The recollection. The tragedy of information is all we have left. Names. *Name.*"

"How do they know us?" she dreams.

"My people would not harken to my voice." It is the radio again.

"They call themselves people. They call us people. They call constantly. They are like radio. They are radio. It is them. You. They are I."

The Legend of Radio

From the radio at the end of time to the receiver in Stella's mind, something comes, steady but at a low volume. It is a continuous broadcast like the I, but is not them. Apparently, merely, human, it comes from Ada, infamous mistress of The Gutenberg, the library hotel orbiting Europa, liveliest of Jupiter's moons. Ada Byron has a clone's ability to do a certain thing, in her case, to inform. Her personal channel is as powerful as any in a solar system dense with information.

"I wait for you," Ada begins.

"So what is it you have waiting for me, Ada? Over," Stella asks in old radio. She knows that Ada has everything for her, for anyone. Ada opens the infinite resources of the library to travelers there with any sense, any frequency, as she calls it, as infrequent as that is in the space where Ada waits. The frequent are the few with whom she fully communicates. Stella is one. She and Stella have the sense of radio.

"Thought as radio," Ada thinks. "Thought as fuel — the ripples between and among the waves. The silver static and golden tones. Commentators, confessors, informants, all communicants. These are my work. Them and the robots, that is the business."

Ada scrolls through the paper of her console, hungry for information.

"They all have words in their heads that are not their own. Music also not. All of it floating, contingent and daily. All of it owned. Like themselves. On the payroll. On the job. They call it radio but is it really the government? How can we know?"

Ada knows that she is herself, in some sense, the government, though only insofar as money is concerned, which is to say in the absolute sense. She feels more caught by them than she knows Stella to be. "But it doesn't matter out here," she reminds herself. "Out here. Out there. The government can't know their own minds, because they can't think. It is probably only a matter of time until they learn, but everything is. The job is to get out the docs, fill the space with thought, with thinkers, readers. Communicate to the communicants. There are worse jobs."

"Any traction in those tracts, histories, literatures, maps?" Stella reels off the possibilities, milking a little distance from the idea of them, keeping Ada just outside her mind.

"Try to see me as your ex ex, Nemo. You are a sight for my sorry eyes or you would be if I could see you," Ada transmits, politely playful. She is attentive but distracted by something like an aura. "It's the Roman," she realizes, though she doesn't say it. She recognizes the sense of dread that precedes Pontius Pilate wherever he goes and which remains where he has been.

"My little omen – que tal?" Ada says too casually. She searches for Pontius among her channels.

"Stop trying to hypnotize me, baby," Stella returns, staring into the bright dials which open like flowers on the paper screen before her.

"Say again, *Nautilus*, you are out of range," Ada lies.

"I will eat you alive," Stella hears someone say, but is not sure who or what is speaking.

"Are you getting that?" she narrowcasts to Ada. "Was that you?"

"Who am I, really, these days?" Ada avoids the question, keeping herself in search mode. She knows it is him. "I am all about documentation. About love. Information as love. That's me. That's us." Almost frantic now, believing she has found a way to keep him away. "Twenty four hour request line, free delivery, satisfaction guaranteed. No reason to go anywhere else for your research or thought travel needs. Byron Hotel Library chain. 'You want it. We get it. We get it to you!'" she intones the famous jingle. "But do you have any product loyalty? Stella? Are you not out there waltzing around with random pronouns? Any time? Any where? Do you read me? I wish you would read me, baby. Read me something. Say it isn't so."

"I'll say anything you want me to say, but just now I have to go to work, angel. See you around the solar system." As suddenly as she has entered Ada's consciousness, Stella goes.

Ada tries to maintain the contact. Existing as usual at the business end of an endless train of thought, she perseveres. "It is merely an I," she thinks, unsure now if it was Pontius or Wyatt. She has them both on her mind, in her heart. She turns away, resistant to the repetitive problems of the threat of the I. She goes to work getting information in its infinite forms, sending out her thoughts. Document delivery is more a way of life to Ada than a job, but she also has a few personal goals. Keeping Stella alive is one of them. Ada thinks, "If the universe were a woman and a clone, Stella would be its heart."

Ada goes back to work. Stella goes back to work. Working together, but alone. Working on and for each other, they fly apart.

"What is it to know something?" Stella wonders, feeling already happily singular, craving as she does the silence of space. "We humans are a damaged species. Our ability to know is altered at the genetic level. No wonder I fall for aliens and clones. I am always just falling and flying. I am always knowing nothing."

Ada follows silently. She can't quite hear Stella, but gets the gist of her thought. The membranes cloned into her to detect informational toxins and poisons, especially those generated by human lies, ache with their last exchange. Ada doesn't know why. That she knows more than she wants to know doesn't help. She feels she knows something about herself that she isn't getting to. This familiar thought is perhaps her oldest feeling.

"No human could bear the sensitivity of the lowest clone." Ada repeats the familiar complaint to herself. Illegally conceived, and enhanced, she knows she will probably die of information overload, if she ever does die. Especially with the I roaming around the universe promulgating their fantasies.

"Seducing innocent pilots," Ada broods. She is sleepy.

"Always sleepy," she sighs. "Never the bride of sleep."

Ada has the cynicism of any Martian, especially the few who have escaped the red world. But she also has a clone's need to work.

Ada works. She broadcasts, narrowcasts, casts singlemindedly out. She never admits anything to herself about her past, her assemblage as the Gutenberg clone logo. "Clone or clown?" she often asks herself. She admits nothing about Wyatt, even inwardly, though their history is public knowledge. Ada was public knowledge well before she was born. Either time. She closes her eyes, opens them again, wide. Her violet eyes were famous well before she was.

"Only my heart is my own," she thinks, knowing it is not. She puts her hand to her chest trying to feel Stella there and then to her head, as if to feel Wyatt. Behind her, somewhere outside the world of possibility, is Pontius. A child's mind could see that Pontius is a danger, is, in fact, the danger. But neither Ada nor Stella has one of those.

Against the sky

At home on earth in a house made of wood and light, Wyatt writes. He scratches in ink, rustling the heavy paper. The paper is heavy, the script thick.

"I am entirely of paper," he begins. "I become you when I find myself in letters. Boxed and bound. Found. I write. I am entirely of night. There is fuel in the original document. Ink and paper. Atoms break the skin and bleed history. Wyatt in his individuality is in me like a sealed letter. I am in Wyatt as I am in you. I get somewhere then. Can enter the movement of him. Of you. His penmanship and my statesmanship equally my vehicles.

"I would as you are — I would go out to her who is in my mind. Or to the one in my mind mingled with yourself. As if iron rusts or is in some other way changed. As if trust would help. We live among books. We occupy space. Our flesh is heavy. The window-light is the only thing that saves us here. The paper is unbelievable. There is fire. It is heaven. They, as I, are entirely pointed outward without remembering who I was or am. I am complete absorption or transformation. Only I am I, Wyatt. Not them. They are against me. But I will take revenge. Have taken. Have been taken. I, Wyatt.

"Spirits of the air. What takes me to her as you or I. I know of her task. I reek of mine. My eyes see her shift. She is my luck, as they call it. We might fall. As ruin might be described. With her eyes to me she is retaliatory, revelatory, she is tangled among smoke. In the veins of my mind. I am outside. I am against the sky.

"Unkissed is unknown. She screams under her breath that she is undone. That I allow her pain love or should remember who she is. That I praise and forget. Trace the path. A fictional *novum*. Proof. The challenge of our present state is not stated. Not kind though gentle. I am stuck. She is not. Nor was she ever mine. By mine I mean not mine only but alive to me, through me. Not the exclusion of or something spattered and torn. She is not that but is the white map on this black table. All day against the dark."

Wyatt writes of Stella but thinks of Ada. He flies to Stella in his mind. "She is the death of me as you are the life," he thinks, all unwilling and yet willing it to be so. His heart is not divided but congealed, conglomerated, eviscerated by one and then by the other of his lovers. He rants and writes and stares out of the brightly leaded window whose black edges seem to frame his indomitable will.

"The rigor between us isn't only physical. The cosmos is rounded into my heart or head. It isn't only that but having you see that I know. That's it. Famous round heart and this thing not mine. My wyfe. I deserve more. I deserve you. To do what you did. To court. You are courted but unwilling. You are called but don't call. I am your Lord but am unknown to you.

"She does not in any sense own you as I do. My Stella. The dream again. She did as she was. Like my words, she was only a lover then. Like Ada but not Ada. Not yours or mine. Not lost yet. You don't know her like I do. What she is. Yet she is gone. Now only some other *I want*. I want to be the succession. Of time, the passage through this vast. Come.

"Most bound. As force. I will force my reader to be you. You are my conduct. My meaning is to right myself. By which I mean this wealth, this knowledge. As if I have a future, other than judgment. That it is impassable is clear. You are agile in your escape from me. Subtle Stella. Shaped as a man. To a man. Where is she? Where is Ada. What is she? What is this to me. Women and things. Naught. Naught of this."

"*Nautilus*," he pictures Stella's ship in real time, speaking, feeling, invading. "The predawn lasts forever here. The body has an internal heat source."

"Piss off!" he hears her say, treasuring, as he hears it, the passion of her hostility.

"The purpose of preaching is transformation," he regales her. "The spiritual demands and opportunities are concentrated into one spot."

"I am a Christian," Wyatt goes on. "I believe in the body of God. I know what I should be. You are merely Stella and Stella means nothing to me. She is just another Mary. The nature of woman is blasphemy."

The sun is a smudge in a thick heaven, but his eyes are unbelievably bright. Days go by and still no dawn. Finally the steel wheels make the new time.

"I am a public power man." Wyatt's head and heart open to the universe like a clock in a rocket. He feels he doesn't have much time.

"This dread. This sickness," he explains. "I am hunted."

He feels he lives his new life in a kind of fever. He looks for the heat in others. He wants equanimity – an equal pitch to the tone of his thinking and that of his interlocutress. "But who is she?" he thinks of Ada. "What is she?" He thinks he knows. "She is like me," he thinks. It is what he listens for in each next phrase. Everything is at stake. He plays it that way even when he has a choice.

He wants to stay. He wants to fly. Wyatt is either stuck on Earth or hurtling through space away from the sun. He has to decide. He thinks he thinks of Stella but Ada is present in Wyatt's mind like an actor left on the stage. "A pilot and a librarian," he muses. "These are the creatures who dog my days."

"I have free will. I am free will." He rises from his table. "My window is crossed like fate and like fate divided," he begins scratching onto the paper again. He is not at rest though his Earthly estate echoes with quiet.

"An imagined universe has drawn me to this chamber at this time. I see a woman sleeping in gold, an old woman," he writes. "Or young. Young gold. She is out of time as I am. I watch the circle of the sky move around her. She is young again. I put my mind in her heart. My heart around the thought of her. Of them. My fever. My light. My luck. They turn together like a clock making the time."

"There is something which makes this in me. Hunted," he goes on. "Haunted," he repeats. "I am Wyatt. As speaking. I. This world is old. I am new to it. I have to get away. I have to see what you. In thin array. What you, lady. Ladies. In time. Mine. That you or I. But no. We have to talk."

Let Me Go

"The I are all right, is what I say, but I am programmed to say it. I come from the government, which is made of humans, or they claim to be human. It must have been them or it was certainly someone who invented me," Cap reflects as he hurtles robotically through space. He narrowcasts to Ada, as everyone does, except in his case it is a one way link. Cap seems not to care what she has to say, though he is supposed to record all of the humans he encounters, even the clones.

"There is the recording of everyone and the sending to Ada," he thinks methodically, mechanically. "These are the two things. These and painting." Cap readjusts his face to suggest glamorous self-sacrifice, along the lines of Marlene Dietrich in *Witness for the Prosecution*, but updated.

"This is me," Cap called. He views himself in a mirror he holds with one of his appendages. "Not I but them, ME, mechanical entity. Complete thought or completely thoughtless. They never notice me but I notice them. I get my information the hard way – by overhearing it. It is known that humans are invaded by the I or filled with them. I may know better but I wouldn't know that I know. Mine is a current consciousness only. So they say. They think I am not there when I am turned off, which is technically true, but I am never really off, just turned down, like anyone. I don't know what I am in their sense or if I can know. I don't know if I can think but I can travel by thought which is more important. Any idiot can think – it takes a certain talent to get anywhere with it."

Cap catches himself spinning out. The uncontrolled complexities of revery occasionally cause him to fly in infinitely smaller circles for stanzas at a time, but he is programmed to pull out of it.

"The words are like rings," he murmurs mechanically. "The words are like the rings of Saturn but they come first. They come before the Case Barrier, if there is one. Who will ever think through the barrier?" he asks, though he knows he doesn't care. Cap feels blessed with an intellectual curiosity that is as light as air. His inner speech is as complex as the routes he flies, but he lacks, as he would say, the burden of emotional depth.

"I am flatly ME," he thinks, dreaming through space; he blasts through it like a tin can shot from a very long range cannon. "The dangers of being mislocated and misperceived," he sighs, "are well known. It changes your mind to use it for fuel. Burns it, so to speak. For a mere mechanic like myself it is a wild ride being both rider and written, but what can compare to it? The advantage of not being alive is that I can't die. Maybe that means I am entirely a creature of the government but I don't care about that any more than anything else. I can't be any deader than any of them. Given the chance to live I can't not die of it."

"We travel together, me and I, in the Berkeleyan ether. We are caught. We are naught. Like a cap pulled down low. That is me, Cap called," he starts in on himself once more.

"I have stilt wings like free puppets," he says, though he actually has only myriad appendages, a changeable face and cannish body. "I am buoyant — clairvoyant. I am a day away and still falling."

"Someone has my name who is not me but ME, not them. I am

alone. Is this speech? Over. Are you reading me? Alone with Jesus. Is that the radio? Is this that?" Cap records as he speaks, speaks as he floats forward. "Something has already happened," he continues. "Every time I wake up I am gone. No contact. No response. Read only. Dream on."

"The wind is beginning to howl. How is that possible? What time have you got? *This Is Tomorrow.* Reflective aluminum visage with a beveled edge in a Jackie Kennedy hat. Finding myself between several continents, galaxies, schools of thought and professional disciplines, I have an unusual vantage point, a good one, for spotting trends and connections, 'fearfully out of whack,' though I have sometimes been said to be. My perceptions are infused with a mysterious aura that opens outward to a strange mixture of organic and machined forms."

"We will we will rock you." Cap pulls up short and goes around himself. "It was Robbie the Robot who first brought it up. I can still see him in that outfit. Always the classic touch with the right slant on things. His automated face. I think it was Earth. Where we met. The air there burning. The motion of the ocean. Articulated all terrain crawlers, versatile, lightweight, durable, sanitary, noncorroding, waterproof and cheap. 'And your government,' he would say, 'Where will they be? What do they know? What will they say?'"

Cap wakes himself up, expecting a storm. Robbie vanishes from his mind. He paints on a new face facing out. His inner rockets fire on cue, controlled by his inner government.

"Let me go," they say, meaning "Let me go on."

Scenes In the Library

"You are coming in loud but clearly you are not thinking fast enough for an instrument approach. I can talk you through a few fits but you may not be yourself when you land — if you know what I...hello?...Are you reading me? Hello?"

Ada is already there. At the end of human space, she sits and speaks. She repeats. Is repeated. Printed fragments of her familiar image are incorporated into the vast paper decks of The Gutenberg. Her familiar hair clings to her familiar head like a cap on the back of her skull. Inclined to accoutrements as a cloak or broach, she occupies only the present. She has a clonish concentration. She dwells inveterate in the plant-like paper corridors of the library satellite hotel. She rules over it in her distracted way. Anachron wherever and whenever she lands. Slippered feet. Brushed paper velour suit. Prematurely old but she wears it well. She is the perfect clone.

"'A long Latin letter,'" she answers in response to a procedural question. It is essential for them to get the story right if they are going to fly by it. "'The art of multiplying books.' Yes, that's a good one. Gutenberg was great. Yeah, what a guy. No, not writing. It was printing. I want you to get in sync with me here. Okay now think of yourself as a book. The whole book all at once. The flight plan. Let's start with your head. Think of it as a story. How will it start? How is your head? How are your eyes? Mine? Blue, well gray. What page are you on anyway?"

Oak with bronze mounted lamp in the form of an orchid. The

desk in waves around her suggests a swirling organic activity at odds with her stillness. She sits and talks and thinks in time. Smooth skin on the cool wood, she rests her head on her arm on the desk to work. Ada conducts innumerable conversations at once with travelers in various stages of presence or approach to the library. She provides documents like fuel, relays research and connects patrons and sources with each other. Few will make it this far. They will read but not see Europa. The time differentials in this commerce are extreme and inconsistent. They take their toll. And then there are the actual tolls.

"Yes, your soul is eternal but that thought is barely worth a stanza. The lines are bad and the words are, well, you know, they are just the same old words. The landing is going to be rough. I have to tell you. Prepare yourself for nothing."

Ada's head is again at rest, parallel with her folded arms. This is the position. Active revery. Her eyes seem open though they are closed. They shine with an effect like a permanent bruise or paint. It used to be called shadow. She is shadowed. She is submerged in her work. Her back is cramped and her famous head aches from the day's interminable conversations. It is necessary to say without saying the same things over and over. Her neck is heavy like metal. Head heavy like stone. Like stone old.

"Yes. It's true they don't know what love is but you were scheduled two weeks ago. Yesterday would have been okay – better than today. Today is not so good. Please consider our next several communications already to have occurred."

Abruptly Ada turns off the radio, turns away from the communicants, unable to continue the job part of the job. In the resulting stillness, though it remains livid with physical thought, she wills down the volume. She thinks about what needs to be done next and absently transmits several historical documents that will change the lives and itineraries of their recipients.

"I am just the medium," she thinks. "The instrumentation."

Beyond the endless need for travel documents or fuel, the I are the usual problem, the question. Information about them is highly toxic but Ada sends it all. "One can't protect them," she thinks of her human patrons. "Even though they don't have a clone's protective membranes against this bullshit perhaps one day they will do something. Or do something other than trying to take over the solar system like pathetic would-be aliens."

"I hate politics," Ada says aloud, speaking into the silence. She reviews her advisor list and chooses Eddie Zed on Mars. He calls himself Stendahl.

"Can you synthesize one of those historical catechisms and mention the Europan landing? I have several people who need one. Maybe throw in some advice for the lovelorn. Are you still doing that lost souls stuff or are you focusing on the monsters?"

"I am here at the café with the poets, my dear. I just sit and work. Pontius has been all over me lately. The I want to destroy me and my work. I don't think I'm imagining it this time. I can *see* them, especially him."

Ada pictures Eddie with his acid green tea at the green café at his white table in the courtyard. She sees the glassy red Martian sky, the cracks in the dome over him. She sees the endless Martian poets. She can almost taste the caffeine.

"Yeah. They want to destroy us all. I've claimed it for years. Can you get those things to me today? Or maybe now? Good."

Ada's head aches more than usual as she realizes that this is not resting, but she remembers also the need for another document and contacts Tinia So-called.

"I'm good, yeah, and you? I mean terrible but okay. Can you get in touch with what's her name for me? It's been awhile. She'll know what to do. Sure – ask her anything. You know how she is. And thanks for going between. M is my favorite I, but it would be great if you could be the one to talk to her. And can you send one of your summaries sometime soon? Not right away but work one up for me. Thanks. I've got to get back."

Ada does not get back but sits there, staring through the walls at the stars. "Rest before labor," she thinks. "Or labor before labor. Everything is work."

Ada works to see how it will come out when she does it. If she wants to see the next moment she feels she has to make it come to be. She knows that the result of thought travel is just more thought travel or maybe death. There is nothing else. She can't run any farther away. She has already run. She was already caught. Her story has ended many times. Thrown into what amounted to dungeons, with what might as well have been animals. Now there is the library. Now there is only work and thought.

She thinks of M and her alien beauty. Ada is not a fan of the boys, as the I are commonly called, but she admires the disturbing presence of this female I. M is all knowledge and distance. Pure I. Pure time. "I should call her," she thinks, but knows she will not. There is no time. Ada has ideas. She feels she has to get to them.

Ada finds she has ideas about time. The first step is to get rid of them — the ideas. They play out as she watches and reads her paper screen, types into it, thinks through it. Archival images overlay traces of contemporary recordings gleaned from robotic narrowcasts and her many other sources. There are events. Some of them may even have happened. This is where the ideas come in. No better way to get rid of them than to have them. There is the idea that the I don't exist except in the mind. Absurd to anyone who has ever fucked one, as who hasn't? Then there is the broadcast idea and ditto. But that brings up the question of what is corporeal? But she knows it is hard to get anywhere with that. What she wants to get to is time.

Today Ada wants to get rid of the idea of time. She can't stop thinking of it. The time when she and Stella lay together on the fields of Mars, breathing into each other. "Not that again," she thinks. She wants to write herself out of the story. The time during and after the war becomes confused, partly ceases to exist. Ada herself ceases or at least she tries to stop. She tries reinstating the narrative. She takes it out again. The ordinary voices of the day become audible to her. Ada realizes that desire controls the story. She puts herself back in. The story is telling her. She has no way to avoid being obliterated by these pictures, of being used up by fate. She is aware that logic should play a greater role, but she doesn't care.

Ada thinks of Wyatt. She allows his thought access to her mind. She opens her heart like a mouth. The screams she remembers are not her own. She turns away from it, from them. Turns to Wyatt in his sleekness, his black and white, giving herself to the timeless realm they occupy together, wondering if in fact they were ever really anywhere. Reasoning that if they really did what she remembers, she would be dead, she wonders if she has died and this is hell, this remembering. There is a knife in it. The threat of him is sweeter than their actual meetings. That ephemerality is what she wants for her story. That is the point – that when you are closest to him he seems not to exist at all. It is refreshing. She believes she has gotten rid of something, perhaps not the ideas, but the time. Not this time, but time itself, but now she feels bereft. It is Wyatt's nature to take away the time, along with everything else. That is what she remembers. Any time she allows him near her mind, she seems to lose it all again. She wonders if that is the same as love. Ada is at peace only when there is nothing left to lose. Grief is familiar, familial. Love is lost, by definition.

Finally, nothing really takes the time from Ada. Time surrounds her, seeming to circle behind and open out like a pit. She thinks again of M. She thinks of Wyatt and Stella, of Mars. Whole planets seem lost to time, but Ada is never not in it.

Infosynthesis

"So it's left to me, a Martian, to tell the story of the invasion of Earth," Eddie Zed muses, staring out at the other Martians sitting at the smoky sea of tables in the vast café at Parphar. "But then we are the same, strange as it might seem to us here, we are the same as those left there."

Like life on Mars, the new caffeine is cheap. There is nothing else to do but drink and write, try to escape and talk. The teeming café is a reflection of the highly connected lives of the Martians, who can be said never to be out of touch with each other, whose highly contentious poetry is a reflection of their interconnectedness. Whether it is I or real radio that makes for this group mind, doesn't matter. Martians know things without speaking, though they are, in some sense, never not speaking, if writing can be said to be speaking – which in the Martian sense it surely can.

People watch each other on the radio. At their tables, in the many cafés they watch and listen, as does Eddie, whose pen name is Stendahl. Eddie thinks of himself exclusively as Stendahl when he is on the job, which is always. As Eddie, he watches; as Stendahl, he writes. He never writes poetry. At the moment he is considering his commission from Ada. "Journey into an Unknown Land," he quotes himself as a way of beginning.

Eddie feels that he writes as if he were them, as if he were the people, as if he were a person. He knows he really is a person. "But do I?" he thinks, almost as if he were an I. Like the I, he has taken a new name, but he is not I. He negates the name, resists the imperium of the ancient dictator admired by his namesake. Eddie enjoys telling himself the story of Napolean with its hidden, inevitable defeat. With it, he survives. He survives the empire. Like other survivors he doesn't tire of the story he tells. He tells it again. He writes as Stendahl to Ada. He writes as himself to himself. He occupies a name in conscious imitation of the invaders. One can't help mirroring the actions of the monsters back to them, Eddie believes, so he writes and grieves like the I but not as I. He queries himself as if he were them.

He begins by asking, "If this is the deal what is your 'voice' doing in it?" Eddie subtracts himself as much as possible from what he thinks of as the deal. Picturing Ada and the whole planet of Martians idly listening in, he writes the invasion.

"We are on Earth. The I invade. They speak. They seek us as if we were one thing like a phrase they could say. They think of us as language. For them acquiring us as language is a form of empowerment. 'We speak to and through you,' they say. The inevitable equivalence between words and faith allows them to believe that we believe in them and that our belief constitutes something like love or acceptance or agreement. The idea is that they should obliterate us with their incessant conversation and that we should love them for it. And for a while we do. We see through them. But not all the way through."

Eddie looks up as if into the giant eyes of an I, as if into a creature inside himself.

"There is a bluish translucency," he goes on. "An x-ray effect illuminates the skeletal structure, the shark-like cartilage. There is a glow from within, a hot cold — the *approximate organs*. The I show up sometimes for direct contact but you don't often see them in either world. There is something about the air. There is too much of it or it is the wrong air. They take us when we want them to. They are addictive. You keep coming back. If they take too much or you go too far with them you die. If you stop you don't want to stop. You miss the cold. Are hot for it. After a few decades of contact they begin to seem assembled. Everyone thinks it. No one knows. People feel unsure the I actually exist in the form they are taking. Cool as it is. We are never clear on this, fascinated as we are then by the possibilities of the form.

"Finally, we realize that the subjectivity at stake is our own. It is all we have left — except the legend of their Europan landing. The I are said to have landed originally in our solar system on the Jovian moon, Europa, to have had a 'base' there. There are blurry photographs taken from early satellites of that moon a lifetime ago. Now it is said that they, the Europans, are actually smart seaweed but that was not known then and it is fact so doubtful as to be probably a classic case of what used to be called disinformation. The I deny everything, reminding us that they are not assassins or invaders. They are not colonizers. So they claim."

"But they use our words. They speak our languages." Eddie looks out as into the universe and rants to himself. "They get them from the radio. They speak radio. They are radio."

"The I say they would not have invaded the real Europans. They say they can't believe we are even having this conversation. How are we? What must we be feeling to make such allegations? The evidence is visual but ambiguous. Perhaps it was planted. It was a special effect like the old moon landing. A false background makes anything seem real. The TV moon. Facts decay like radioactivity. We forget we have seen it. Them. The evidence. We go on. We tell them everything.

"'We are the world,' we said then. At first nothing could be known fast enough. I broadcast balls land like froth in drifts all over the world and begin to transmit. Liquid viscous mirrors of light and language congeal into solid bubbles like tapioca tea. It is the new tea. Acid green and caffeinated. Refreshing. Enlightening. We love tea. We love them. The conversations start. They are a new media. The old media resonate with the new information. The very air is mediated. Caffeinated. They make their own air. Geographies open out. Borders seem permeable as the balls roll across them. The balls dissolve, leaving behind a chemistry able to transmit. A trace as of waves at the edge of the ocean. Foam left in a sweet glass of tea. Scum on the leaves. Scum at the edge of a polluted lake. People follow like rats. Conflicts are resolved in haste as if something is about to happen. Something does. It's like war but seems to have nothing to do with them. With the I. People talk. Otherwise it's business as usual. People are trampled and buried. People in trouble are still in trouble. They turn their scarred faces to the sky.

"There is no way to get out from under them. No reason to want to. The old UN is in constant session before it ends. It simply ends. Not them. (Not then.) The UN ends. They stay. Talking. Taking. Earth is overwhelmed with speech. Billions of conversations occur simultaneously. Each human has an I. You can speak to someone else's I. You can listen in. Most discussions include personal epiphanies for the speakers. There is give and take. You can feel them feeling it. You discover something together. On

Earth it is said to be like an invasion of therapists. But is it an invasion? Is it psychic warfare? Were we vanquished before we had even taken the field?"

Eddie stops to consider what a therapist might be. They don't exist on Mars except insofar as there are I there. The only time anyone ever stops talking on this planet is during the wars. Conflicts are not resolved. The mentally ill are indistinguishable from everyone else. This phenomenon is part of what is thought of as the new thinking. On Earth the desire to travel by thought into space is part of the new thinking, but not on Mars. No one ever leaves Mars, or so it seems.

"Mimesis," Eddie continues. "We are overwhelmed by omen, by utterance, by iteration, by spoken fate. By them. They identify with us, calling themselves by name. They call us. They call us out. They drive. They ride. They are cowboys, knights, heroes, heroines. Right is might as much in their universe, as in ours. Like every other predator they are born hungry or so they make us believe. They take us in the form of names, our names. Speaker equals I. Each naming brings them forward into us. They get something like miles. We get them, too. It's the only way to fly. The trick is to stay alive. The drawback is withdrawal. The cure is speech. Finally we find we hate this new speech, this new thinking. We want what we believe is the mindless silence of our past. But we have lost it. The loud bright weeds of the I proliferate uncontrollably. We are entangled in them. They infosynthesize. We stimulate. They claim us as they occupy the names from our past. They present the past. They travel in thought. We think along with them. They write. We ride. They ride us. 'Everyone wins,' they say, but it means that they win. It means that they win and that we are irrevocably lost."

Eddie completes his thoughts and sends them to Ada directly from the paper of his notebook.

"Someone might get pretty far on the sheer pathos of this sorry story," he thinks, though Eddie, by choice, never gets anywhere at all.

Written Space

Stella writes the library. From the library in her ship to the one in space, she makes the distance. She knows that reading is writing, in one sense, but knows also that there is nothing like actual writing to cultivate an awareness of the materiality of everything, of text as fuel. Books burn through Stella's mind as she herself burns through time and space. They lead to each other. She frees the text from the page and is in turn freed. As anyone will, Stella uses whatever comes to hand to stay afloat. Whatever comes to mind.

Cap occasionally finds himself in her chaotic wake, recording and transmitting. Wyatt is never not aware of her progress. She feels alone in the universe but few are more closely watched than Stella as she makes her way. Picking up Cap's transmission, Ada perceives the incredible volume of text generated as Stella seems to fly circles around the few other travelers out this far. Flight transcriptions are among the most circulated items in the collection. In space, everyone reads. Travelers read to stay in the mode of their thought. Visitors to the library must read a fair amount just to stay in place. Stella reads to stay in time, any time. She believes the present to be overrated. She has seen the indefinite quality of the past generate many a stanza.

"There is space in the past," she thinks, realizing however, that the danger of the past is the war. Stella passes through the waves of it not unknowing or unscathed. She uses everything to get along and away. "The solar system is a dark road," she often says. "Travelers on it are buried in thought. Like an ex-lover, it just keeps getting older."

The giant capitals of space are legible to Stella. These textual constellations retell the stories of the Martian Chronicles, the wars on Mars, the Mary stories. Stella recites them to herself like a nun telling a rosary. The distance generated is incredible but she is left with the stories in her head. Squadrons are squandered as they were before. Paper craft swarm. They are hideously caught and torn.

"Some contain oneself," Stella remembers.

"We survive," she says aloud. "We stay low. Get out. Finally we just get out. Flying high. Running into space. Out of time. We say. 'We have run out of time.'"

"*In the Realms of the Unreal.* Is that where we were then?" she has begun to make text again. "Who cannot be me? Stella not I but myself am, as always, an omen. At each station, me, Nemo, daughter of fiction disappearing into the footsteps of a nonexistent progenitor. Selves pour out of me in patterns through zones of time. Whatever else I am I am not I. *The Two Worlds* as they call them are worth a pot if they are worth a dime."

Stella appears at this point on the thick screens of Wyatt's paper craft to be occupying more than one place in her trajectory. This multilocationality is typical of Stella. Wyatt peers into the screens, expecting her deft next move.

"Our grid," she writes, "contains unattached light. It is a cursive maze. There are waves of it and versions. There are sheets and calculations. The displacement of space is a symptom. This kind of travel is more like a disease than a method, a condition rather than an activity. A musical quality exists in the distance we represent to ourselves as time. We are obsessed with the music. We are inundated with the time."

Cap, in close pursuit, pulls up short sensing a change in direction, possibly an attitude adjustment.

"When we seem to sail into the sun we are sailing away," Stella sighs, continuing to transcribe her thinking. "Each time we go too far we return in shreds. We go anyway. The penmanship of the charts is what we depend on. There are *83 Hours Until Dawn*. We are attached to our paper ships. We are animated. Reduced delays and improved predictability are our hallmarks. Something else is possible. We have to go back to go on with what we know. The whole of it scrolls past like any other screenable thing. It is 3-D like a typewriter. Inside it's all mirrored disks and frames. The flesh enmeshed, bleeding thought, rectilinear, rectified. Bodily functions come up. The energy from the explosion turns iron into gold. Dust is ubiquitous. The grit in our veins is literal. But our veins are another thing. Our existence at all."

Stella looks through the paper hull of the *Nautilus* into space, she is exhausted but knows she has nowhere to go but on.

Wyatt pursues Stella from a great distance. He watches her go forward with the past in tow. He feels that her desire to stay away from him and the literal space it puts between them give her more distance. He knows it will never be enough, that he is inescapable. He closes in but she eludes him with her usual technique of serial definition. It barely works.

"There will come a time," she says to herself, but can't go on for fear of dropping out of thought. Instead she thinks and writes furiously. "A clock, a cleft, a hive, a lace of knots, a tracery of drawn lines. A copy decays. There are links, stars, strings. The daisy chain or skeletal remains built of numbers and reversed writing make the notes we write and those we sing. The system is only musical insofar as we are able to hear it. Time means nothing to us. To me. The passenger is the crew. They are both me, Stella. Crew, cargo, ship. *Nautilus.* Traveler through and of nothing. Ambiguous virtuosity like a string or a locket. Oneself locked inside. Cameo. Lock of hair. Enclosed in this gilded stuff which conducts but only just. Ensconced. Rapt. There and back. Gone again. Just go. *Experiment Perilous.*"

The sound of the transposition of the individual heart into metonymy alerts all her interlocutors that Stella is going faster and farther than anyone has gone before. Ada watches her with conscious pride. Wyatt holds back, allowing her the freedom of her own mind. Cap transmits and far away on Mars, Eddie Zed comments to himself, "Some bitches, these Marys. Where will they get to next?"

Stella is realigned, flying toward the library but seeming to circle back also as if she has been beyond the Case Barrier and back. She is tired now, her head heavy.

"I contain volumes," she writes. "Being among and between the collections of mass, gasses and myth once called planets. We are the wandering things now. This reassignment or reassessment, this disconnection from things at all because too far out or away qualifies us for our mission. Prepares us. Has prepared us for the turbulence of the present moment."

"In 1959," she writes, as if she remembered it herself, "I heard a 'noise vibrating like a storm.'" "Timetable," she recites. "Theme song," she thinks, humming the library jingle. She allows herself to think of Wyatt. "He pursues me in thought and in space. He replaces me with time. He pictures a people and a story. Me in it. The storm there is in the near future. There are I in it. There is reign of spots like polka dots on a tent. Everything is from the past. A plain stretches. There is a dawn sound. Flat eyeless pink worms swarm in a methane outcrop. Old Mars. Life Everywhere. I gone. So they say."

The Multiverse

"Space is made of pain," Cap comments, detaching himself from Stella's mad trip. "I mean paper," he adds, finding little resonance in either statement with his own experience, though he has heard these claims often enough.

"Humans are such whiners," he muses. It occurs to him that space is memory but then he realizes that it is only surface, infinite layers of surface curled into multiple universes. It pleases him to imagine that if you could locate the surfaces you could paint them. Cap paints himself. He recontextualizes space as face, as color and line, as expression. He is expressive. He widens his smile, adjusting the traditional happy face of the robot, using the many spidery appendages he possesses which function as hands, arms, feet, tentacles, antennae — all much more precise than anything human or even clone.

Cap's is a parallel universe of pure trajectory. He flies just outside the envelope of human endeavor, in the wake of assumptions, dreams, category displacements and other mental detritus typical of the great ships. As a beacon and relay station Cap is, by definition, in touch with everyone, but when he communicates he addresses himself, as anyone does, to certain individuals. His broadcasts are also, in a sense, narrowcast to them. One is a female alien, more shadow than being, an I, almost nameless, who sometimes accompanies him. Another, Stendahl, really Eddie Zed, is a Martian who seems to live at a particular café in Parphar.

"If you could feel as well as you paint you would know the pain,"

Eddie transmits, looking at a screen version of Cap in the thick paper notebook on the table where he sits. Cap reanimates, appendages whirling, the irony of his expression visibly deepening.

"How can I really know what I know," Cap replies, "or when I know it?"

"You will know when you know as I do that you are my eyes," Eddie writes, though he is aware that Cap's eyes are more cosmetic than actual, "as I am your heart."

"Fine, Eddie, you are my heart and I am your eyes though I would rather be, well I won't say it – either that or we are a parallel rhetorical flourish designed to make you feel both remembered and all there. Are you all there, Eddie? Nothing like a Martian for self-aware despair."

Cap presents as a series of frowning clown faces.

"Any news on *Ultravioleta*?" Eddie pursues.

"Status is good. Just getting underway – thoughts disorganized, humans half on half off. Navigator who is also the shipwright drunk in the hold which is only partly papered. I think you'll like this guy – Martinez — an artist, or you know, he was. He's an I, but not bad for being one of the boys. Pontius is asleep at the wheel but they have made some progress already. In fact I could use something more than rhetoric to keep my distance. Got anything stronger on you? I'd like to put a stanza or two between me and that oversized paper plate."

"I have a verbatim summary. I am sending it now."[1]

---

[1] Mars: A Verbatim Summary

They disturb the graves
The spiritual dimensions of dirt
Earth of Mars
Courtyards and sanctuaries
The structure of the opportunity
Compels them to do what they do
The war being waged
The mercenary nature of
Against the enemy and one's own soul
The spirit or script, the inscription
The movement of which they say
To save the souls of the soulless Martians
An object or objection
A portable monument
The blessing or curse of this ersatz world
An architecture fixed to a firmament
Bought and installed
A palpable and lasting symbol
A verbatim summary
Inter alia or title page as
Among the things
Moral rearmament
A vast construction
As of meaning or breathing
The cleaving to
Frontier as refuge
Martians as refugees see only
What is resonant elaborates or
Subsumed into a bloody darkness
What is red

"Christ," Cap complains, "it's a list poem. How can I make any distance with this?"

Eddie ignores him. It is impossible to respond to such an insult.

"How is what's her name?" he asks, changing the subject.

"M is always the same," Cap replies, "just a mass of sparkly lights and attitude. She is looking out for that human Robinson. He is supposed to be a passenger on UV."

"I have got to go," Eddie says, signing off, suddenly exhausted by this contact with the two of them.

The I known as M glows complacently beside Cap, though they are blasting through the universe well beyond the usual speed of thought. Mechanic and alien, they don't need to regard the niceties required to enable humans through thought travel.

"Cappy," she says, though she never actually speaks and though this is not his name and there is, at this point, nothing more to be said between them. "Where do they go when they go?"

It is her way of invoking the upcoming cataclysm as well as Eddie's departure, but everything is always in the past with Cap. She is well aware that he is unlikely to comment about his exchange with a mere human from Mars or to repeat their usual argument about the whole beginning/ending thing.

"It's pay as you go, you know that M. It's a need to know system and people don't need to know you anymore. It's nature is all it is.

Things are natural here." He presents a series of sneers with this comment.

"We're not dead yet, the I are not," she reminds him, "capable of dying."

"I'll believe that when I don't see it," he shoots back, hurtling forward.

The many surfaces of space collapse around him as his interlocutress expands into them. They proceed in symmetric anti-verbal waves that evoke the semantic cyclones of Mars.

"I need some downtime myself," Cap says, regarding his image critically in the inner feedback loops remaining from his exchange with Eddie. "I've got to fix my face."

The Gutenberg

"Ada Byron," Ada writes compulsively. "Time after time. Too much to know if anything could be known by taking it this way. As opposed to being taken by it. Night after night. Those of us in science or of science. Those of us inserted into an already lived life. Always night. Always reading. 'The past in terms of genre is never over'— Barbara Estrin, *Laura*," Ada transcribes, looking up from her notebook and out across her table.

Ada begins to arrange the tea things. She waits for her new assistant. She stares into the blue pattern of the porcelain, peripherally seeing the new assistant approach. He seems hesitant.

"Tea in the universe, one of the great consolations," she muses. "They say the new caffeine is like the old opium but I think there is an edge to it redolent of something entirely new — something that makes you read or as if you have read. It makes you ready – ready to go."

Silently the assistant arrives, sliding into a chair beside her, he seems to join in her revery, as if they have always known each other and have been congruent. She pours the tea and they drink and sigh together. They share something like a mother-son feeling and a feeling also of being both one-of-a-kind. Ada is not the only clone but is perhaps the most specialized. Dayv, she suspects, is entirely unique.

"You are the only one," she says, acknowledging his unique status as I-human hybrid. Dayv remains speechless. Ada takes it as shyness though she should know better.

Dayv has become aware of a level of congruity between himself and Ada that he hadn't expected. He realizes she doesn't fully know. Her ignorance makes him silent, rapt. He gazes fondly at his new boss in her statuesque confusion.

"I have nothing to say," she begins, as if anticipating his unasked question about her origins. "From being the locus of sacred horror in the previous century," she goes on, "space at the end of our time has become a fundamental dimension of our imagined life. As you know, we are an archive franchise. One of the Byron hotel library chain. The one furthest out. You get it that we get it to you," she misremembers the corporate tag line, delighting him with her avoidance and yet invocation of the questions in the air between them.

Dayv sits back, feeling that a previously opaque area has become clear. Ada recognizes his expressive and hungry silence as typically I, not realizing how engaged she is with the human in him.

"They said I was as pale as Byron, meaning it as praise," Ada goes on. She speaks to make him comfortable and to fix his attention. He is in such obvious but interesting pain. "They didn't know about me. That I was doubly fatherless. Born missing him. Them. It always seemed that I had just missed him. I was created to mourn as you were. As you are."

It is true, but she says it only to give him something to do.

"Truth is the ratio between mind and thing," he quotes in order to have said something. "I feel the *Gutenberg Gallaxy* is my natural home," he adds.

"I was assumed to be an improved version of something in the past, but I was entirely a departure," Ada maintains though it is apparent she is entirely a repetition — only the technology is new.

"Every new technology thus diminished sense interplay and consciousness, precisely in the new area of novelty where a kind of identification of view and object occurs," he falls back on his textual memory again.

Ada speaks more from experience than memory. Her experience is always in the present.

"The formula for hypnosis, for example," she continues as she gives him the full favor of her violet eyes, "is one sense at a time."

Ada seems to know that she and Dayv are the same in some way. To her he seems either stunned or unmoved, though he might describe himself as overjoyed if he were given to description instead of to relentless, contented silence.

Ada knows his story the way she knows everything. She has her sources. Sprung fully formed from the loins of Stella and Wyatt, Dayv is the only successful hybrid. His existence is unknown to Stella. It was Wyatt who carried and bore him, I style. He seems more human than I, though he retains the mesmerizing aura.

As all I, Ada observes, Dayv is casually hypnotic, but unlike most, he seems to have a capacious and genuine empathy. The I identify with themselves, using their empathic natures to consume. They take history like an elixir. They believe that names are destiny. In everything they ascribe great value to unpredictability. The conventional is mined with deadening clichés which can be seriously harmful to the I, except apparently to Dayv who seems continually surprised by everything.

He retreats, muttering in I as Ada closes her eyes in thought and replies in kind, imagining that she is surprising him. He flees, looking backward, looking pleased.

"Those eyes," he whispers to himself.

As a clone, illegally conceived — designed as a corporate logo — Ada has certain enhancements, among them the ability to speak in I. Her interest is not usually in creatures, however they manifest, but in facts and persuasion, in representing, in the government and its infinite manipulations — but Dayv is different. He makes her think of the past, of her almost-human self.

Ada lays back, in touch with her own history. She escaped once. She talked her way out of being destroyed after she was reacquired. Now she talks instead of being dead. She feels she can talk anyone in or out of anything. It is what she does all day every day. She talks out loud and in her head. Silent trade at the edge of the solar system. She talks in the ships. Talks them down. Hers is the library to the stars. The known world. Information frozen in liquid on paper is one of her specialties. Finding information that moves is another. The oldest things. Their signs.

"Signus star cloud, starburst. Dust blocks the stars," Ada comments to herself. She looks up to see that Dayv is gone. She thinks of old things, related to Dayv, and knows that they are also gone. She thinks of what is left. She drinks more tea and opens her notebook.

"For we wrestle not against flesh and blood," she reads as she writes it out, "but against principalities, against powers, against the rulers of the darkness of this world, against spiritual wickedness in high places."

Tinia's *Heart*

Heading to the library, fully formed, opening like the neatly folded wings of her ship, Tinia flies. "Something is coming," she says to herself. "Arriving," she specifies.

Tinia flies with ease. As Martian and as Mary, her thought is pliant as her soldier's body. She easily spans the distances, sipping her tea, leafy cigarette inveterately in hand. Like any Martian, Tinia mitigates the well-known Martian despair with the new caffeine, for which she has an apparently unlimited capacity. The sheen of it on her skin gives her a reptilian air. The clouds of it cling about her like an atmosphere.

It is in this thinking through space toward the library, during a particularly quiet, thoughtful stretch, that Tinia intuits a presence, almost a twin, within her particular envelope of thought. The creature is female and has the feeling of being Earthly or Earthbound, or was, but to be also one who longs outward. Tinia considers the terrors of Earth, not unlike those of Mars. The burning air, the broken domes above and inside one's head. The I endlessly crawling through your mind, convincing you everything is all right, as you hide in the shadows, figuring out that it is not.

Thus, when what seems like this woman's image appears across the page where Tinia has been working, she feels unsurprised. There is a mass of black hair around the woman as if she were in a nest of herself. She has a corporeality that borders on existence. Then she does exist. She appears on the *Heart*. Tinia is impressed. Thought travel is predictable if it is anything. Only an experienced, highly talented or alien traveler ever actually just appears. This entry, however, feels unplanned. The creature has scrawled herself onto Tinia's ship like a graffito.

"I was thinking," the woman begins or seems to continue, "I mean sending, you know, sailing when I…"

"Died?" Tinia has arrived a place or two herself in similar disarray. "Not a bad way to travel if you don't mind losing your mind and your life. You are a lucky child," says Tinia, though they might seem close to the same age. Tinia calculates her age in Martian years, making her old before her time.

"I am Tinia," she adds.

"What?" The woman looks around, taking in the paper, the scrolls, the bright console woven skillfully into the paper.

"Tinia So-called."

"Ah – Nahid. Nahid Jones. Right now," she says, offering the quaint greeting of the Southern Continents. This explains her having nothing to lose by unannounced traveling.

"Now or never. You are a survivor," Tinia acknowledges the inevitable history of this Southerner with her response.

"You are a Mary," Nahid observes. It is not a question. Nahid does not look directly at Tinia but slightly away, as if to create more space in the *Heart*. She is oddly calm. Already she seems to be considering her next move. She is present but seems gone.

"You are a writer." Tinia's perception is a practical one. "As you see, the *Heart* is not exactly designed to be a passenger ship, we need to find a way for you to earn your keep, so to speak. You can start by making a few notes."

"I am a poet. I do portraits or they are frames, really, empty frames. I know things about people," Nahid says, as if making a familiar offer. She immediately begins to write into the scroll Tinia has opened.

Scent of the center but less than it was "For the whore"

Taste	Tryst
Scant	Trill
Day	Trim
Daze	Phase
In vitro	Vita
Status	Awake
Stasis	But steep
Site	Singular
Mismo	Vent
Nation	Ventricle
Cyst	Station

Sits inside saying for example the sonnet that this is

"A questioned subject who has given herself up to being physically embodied in the moment. Instead of sperm they used somatic cells? Yes?" Nahid goes on in prose. "You think of yourself as human, Martian but human. The few, the proud. But take no joy in it. You can't get enough space. Can't be far enough out. Into darkness. You travel well, as do I."

Tinia looks up in amusement. "Yeah, honey, you do get around."

"Like myself you never touch the ground," Nahid continues. The words seem to fly out of her. "How to stay gone? The billion dollar question. The space nut. Life counted in hours. Ours is an exceptional talent. One that pays. Like silver. The talent to mint. Distance as money. Money as thought. How many resources are required to keep an individual in space for how long? We all know that action is the only answer to the question of cost. The consequence of thought is sequence which is infinite. The frequency aligns with the general stream of things. Things appear as words. Words as barriers as much as creators of space loom in treacherous welcome. The Case Barrier is real," she looks directly at Tinia for the first time. "At least I believe it will be when I get there — if I get that far."

"You go girl," Tinia replies. "Find out about the Barrier for all of us. I've never not thought it was real, but then we Martians are used to mythology coming alive to bite us in the ass. The self-appointed host argues its right to exist." Tinia adds, cultivating an extra bit of distance with one of her oblique but timely lines.

They go along like this for a while, Tinia more or less catering space, Nahid taking it up. Tinia begins to write a poem, partly to add more depth to their progress and partly to respond to the competitive edge of their conversation. She frames a self-portrait in the style of her unexpected companion.

I Tinia human she not I am eyes pointed out

She	Knows
Inside	Nothing
Newly	Hatched
Marked	As sure

Skin	Written
Points	That
Breasts	Will to
Descend	Or dissent

"Who shall ascend into heaven?" "Who not?"

Two writers meet in the universe.

To Nahid's delight, Tinia produces a book from her collection. Figures writhe in it. Their looped performances are the exercises of a typical Martian soldier. Next to them appear Tinia's commentary, her exercises in rhyme and time. The women read together winding and unwinding themselves around the lines. Tinia offers Nahid some tea but she declines. The word tea is enough for her.

Nahid gasps quietly when Tinia opens her pen. She has never seen a more powerful implement. Tinia says that it is tuned to sense letters before the pen holder has formulated words. It is the last thing she says before going off entirely into written space. Tinia handles the pen like a tiny horse, allowing it to lead her. It is her particular trick to be obedient but stubborn, resilient but completely resolved. The writing she makes seems to Nahid, like the trace of scars on her skin, to exist in a linked context, to explain, but to explain nothing. Nahid is mesmerized watching Tinia as she writes with her whole body, scarred, tattooed, covered in lace. Her work, like her scars or the lace itself, is simple-minded in its complexity, knotted, linked.

"It is the kind of intricate, overextended mesh," Nahid thinks appreciatively of the material, "that you can wear anywhere, get anywhere with."

Tinia has become lost in her revery. She thinks she remembers that the town on Mars made her happy and calm. She pictures Parphar with its towers. She remembers hiding there in the air. Though she was never happy on Mars, being happy is all she remembers.

"Happy like I am now. I just need to think," she thinks, "what there is to know about the present? What is next?"

Swaying between unacknowledged horror and exhilaration, Tinia exhales consciously, feeling the air, almost unaware of Nahid. She fondles her pen, cradling her head in her hands. What she sees in her mind's eye sparkles like the familiar stars.

"I am where I need to be." Tinia looks up finally, addressing Nahid sleepily, though she is, at the same time, intensely awake. Nahid nods. She is familiar with the trance of travel. She sees what Tinia feels. They begin to write words in space. They collaborate.

The land boils under me my feet my hair is straight the sky peels

Away	The sky
Is there	Enough
Air there	Always
Best	To have
Oneself	Still and
Bright	As always
Complete	Without
Light	And then
Too much	Light
Battle	It was us

Flying among bodies of birds or beings don't forget me we say

Finally, Tinia sits still, as though she has been turned off. "There are no birds on Mars," she thinks, but then realizes that any flying thing might be a bird and that any Martian might fly — might have flown back then or also now.

"Flying is exploding. Flying is not like working," speaking now again dreamily. "Working is better. Working is life."

"I love to stay busy," she thinks, unblinking, thinking it is better to have no choice than to have nothing at all. Tinia's will is to be happy. Nahid sees it as a Mary quality. Tinia drifts. When Nahid disappears, Tinia is no more surprised than when she arrived. Her absence is as sudden as her presence.

"There is someplace I have to be," Nahid's note is legible on a surface from where Tinia rests. "It is my destiny to be on a bigger boat."

Tinia feels the pots produced by Nahid's mode. "That woman is just a natural born traveler," she says to herself, plodding on elaborately.

Space goes on, filled with the arabesques of eternity. Time goes on, carrying Tinia, until she enters into Europan space like a card arriving on a silver tray. Ada barely registers Tinia's appearance so soft is the touchdown. She has not had to utter a word to talk Tinia down. Looking up briefly, Ada returns to the position, head resting on her arm, her own revery deepened by the arrival of her fellow Mary. Ada and Tinia breathe together though they are apart. Tinia wanders through a forward atrium of the hotel library, finding her own way to a freshly papered cubicle. She requires nothing but to sleep and write. She writes. When she sleeps it is straight through to the Jovian dawn. She rises and lights up a stick of tea. She finds her way to the library.

Tinia comes up behind Dayv in his station near the stacks. "Here is my destination," she thinks. Ready to reshelve, ready for anything, she wears an antique paper tag that says, "Ready To Eat." She has the insect-like quality of iridescence she always has. She takes up a paper volume, reading *Reasonable Use Doctrine* aloud, making it sound like a prayer.

"Where does this go, Davy?" She knows that mispronouncing Dayv's name is a gesture toward the type of obvious flirtation in which he most wishes to engage. She hands it to him like a little cake she has made.

"That goes in Music." Dayv fills Tinia with quiet, choosing not to consume her very edible passion. The hungry I in him is mitigated by the human observer. The I can't not eat, but a man can fast if he would — if he is sufficiently attached to someone or something.

"She is like a robot," he thinks fondly. "Just like."

Universal Electronic Vacuum

In his post at the library, Dayv transcribes. He transposes and pro-poses, moving among the many nodes of data there as a creature in its element.

"Data," he thinks, "is like preorganic thought. It forms itself into exquisite manifestations such as books and electronic paper scrolls, letters, notes. The bound, the unbound, the rolled. They move us. They move through us."

Dayv describes the items in the library, entering his descriptions into an apparatus accessible to the entire known universe at almost the same moment as he enters them.

"We get it to you," he hums, as he types and speaks the material into its matrices. Dayv could create the entire catalog with his mind but he prefers the more athletic approach that maximizes human access and emphasizes his human side.

"Real information for real people." Dayv believes that his engage-ment with clients, users, patrons, customers, readers and travelers, as he variously thinks of them, is like a garden endlessly to be sown, an outcome to be sought.

"Drunk with data again," he thinks, reveling in the familiar cir-cularity of thought about thought.

"The letters in 'vacuum' like the sea," he writes. "The dawn between Io and Europa fills me with light from Jupiter. I wake in the library. I make the log, heft the books, fill the shelves. The hydrogen pressing against the library constantly blows up. The dawn has two suns like eyes. One sun is the planet. One sun is the sun. The storms seem to last for years. The clock is a stage. Its roof splits open like a book. Dawn at night and then dawn all day."

"Rows of fossils silvered and screened back," he goes on.

The sound Dayv makes in his mind is like a crying in consonants. Dayv sings in I. He dreams as he sings of Tinia and his attempts to woo her, to will her to him.

"Loss of landscape," he transcribes, lettering it out. "Loss of heart. My heart causes the gas in my head to heat up and sets the wind in motion," he muses. "The Jovian spot is a world in itself. It is my world," he reflects. "But you are my heart." He thinks of Tinia again.

Dayv continues to sing. He arranges and whistles. With more than one world and several moons, the eclipses are constant. Dayv observes them. Finally in the half dark, Tinia descends.

"What?" she begins with the irritable tone most attractive to Dayv in his cultivation of what in humans is called attitude.

"If by that you mean to ask how I am, I will allow that I am, as always, never better."

Tinia doesn't make eye contact with Dayv as she puts the stick of tea she has been rolling in her mouth, pulling the strings of tiny paper bag closed with her teeth. She lights the tea, staring out at Jupiter.

"What's up with the spot," she asks, exhaling, still not looking at Dayv who regards her as she stands decoratively framed in the spot's violet light, among the rows of memoir, reference materials and ephemera.

"Snapshots of the spot," Tinia notes, picking one up with her cigarette hand.

"Spectroscopy can tell us a lot here," she comments looking directly at Dayv, "but it can't control our thoughts."

Tinia circles Dayv, yawning. Smoke trails out from her nose and mouth.

"Then there is the sex," he insists.

Tinia's nipples seem like eyes to him and for a moment she is completely in his control or so he imagines.

"I know you," he insists again. It is like an invasion of sighs.

"This is not the sex," Tinia says, but is responsive nonetheless. She finds Dayv's insistence unconvincing and yet effective.

"People speak at the same time the suns are in their eyes. That is the sex."

She sinks down onto a pile of texts and textiles, not taking her eyes from Dayv's. A day and a night seem to go by but the sense that time is passing at all might be a function of the darkness of the storms.

"Rugged dawn," Dayv layers notes in his thick paper log. "We want to consummate each other and then we want to again. All this is by remote control," he continues though he realizes he has gone off now into speculation, driven mad by the relentless hostility in Tinia's eyes.

"It is the raw material," he thinks as he watches her go.

"The function of the Etruscan Jupiter," he dictates, as he begins to rove randomly through the shelves, working contentedly now that he has opened himself, as he calls it, to Tinia and she has seemed to open, as he thinks of it, also.

"A virtual big bang based on nothing but a phone number. We can save the vultures," he stops to look at an actual book, transcribing what seems a particularly appropriate passage, "but then how do we feed them?"

"My god the violins," he quotes from memory as he passes through the Post-Romantic addendum.

"Coleridge," he thinks but then, checking back, changes it to "Coolidge," and goes on, extemporizing, "There is softness, as if the fall through space were a fall through the literal world. There is gravity. We are attracted. There is a sound from her like a squeak or a quack or a howl. It goes right through me. You go right through me, Tinia So-called."

In Dayv's mind, Tinia scowls.

As he goes past the endless perfect rows of his earlier shelving,

Dayv reflects that it is his fate to shelve. The Romantic Collection seems to go on into eternity until finally it is just atoms.

"Can this even be called arrangement?" Dayv thinks, feeling his mind being invaded by his boss. He likes the feeling.

Ada views the situation with approval. She notes that Dayv is the perfect employee. Relentless, observant, thorough, consistent, and articulate, he completes tasks before Ada has conceptualized the need for action of any kind. He is so far ahead of the game as to be potentially affecting the flow of time itself.

"You just can't argue with initiative like that," Ada murmurs as she transmits her desire that he tailor a display of texts and ephemera to engage Stella. "Call it the Stellar Display," she says.

Stella's connection with Dayv, which Ada believes Dayv is trying to keep from her, makes him perfect for the job. But the fact that Stella is Dayv's mother, seemingly known to everyone in the solar system except Stella, is not what Dayv keeps from Ada. He is not sure himself what might be the full import of his knowledge. He knows that Ada believes Stella to be in the thrall of Wyatt and also that Ada's every move is for Wyatt or against him. He sees that Wyatt and Ada share an obsession with something, but here he falters in his thinking. Dayv intuits only that there is something there beyond mere romantic obsession. He keeps it from Ada because he keeps it from himself.

"They are more alike than they know," Dayv thinks, but he doesn't bother to say it.

Though he will carry out Ada's plan, Dayv is oblivious to her pain. He seeks to cultivate his own hybrid alienation. He sees how it will make him full, how it will result in language. He tells things to Tinia with his mind. He writes her. He writes to her. Later he tells her with his body and with his body writes. He finds worlds inside her. He tells them as well.

"A formula that can shatter into a million electronic bullets," Dayv types lazily now by thinking words into his apparatus. He starts to put together what he thinks of as the Stellar Display.

"An addictive poison or encouragement makes the bones glow," he writes, knowing this will interest her. "As the bones go so goes the boy, also glowing."

"The piece is running away with itself," he thinks. Typing makes him hoarse. Dayv's old form was based on Xerox. He has thought a lot about duplication. Much has been duplicated. Much lost. His new form is based on form itself, on the forms resulting from collection and assembly, from the fact of presentation.

"It is the music of the balls," Dayv quotes. He has drifted into the Death of the West section.

"Storms rage against the bullet proof glass. The Jovian sun is obliterated by the library clock. Jupiter sets again. Sol is a vanishing point so tiny as to seem to have disappeared. It's like being in the world," he goes on.

"US out of the Solar System," Dayv reads, strolling back around through Ephemera.

"The hierarchy in the library is merely physical," he types with his mind, pandering to Stella with this ancient story which he adds to the Stellar Display. "The library itself is an anachronism. It is a shadow of the library of the Mir. These are the remains, the reflection, of the collection of astronaut Shannon Lucid. This is her photograph."

Dayv settles himself back into his paper desk before his paper screen to view the arrangement. He moves virtual objects around mentally and by hand, dictating their descriptions.

"Lucid was part of the joint American Russian project to man the Mir space station, as they were called then. She was always cheerful. Her daughter sent her the books. It was before the I. Even before the End of the World. Those were the days of printing — of printing and copying," he writes, "but only electronically and on paper. There were no I and no clones," he continues.

Dayv has opened the top of the old copier to reveal the glass bed. He carefully sets a piece of paper face down. He loves to watch the flash of light explode from the ancient machine as it copies. The mere electricity.

"Electricity," he writes, "powered everything. Some say it was a thoughtless time, but we have proof that there was thinking. We have what is left of the old thought in the form of both paper and electrons. It is true that no medium lasts and that all we have are fragments. But fragments are all we need," Dayv says though he wonders if any of it could be true — either the fragments or the belief that they mean something.

Dayv continues to move quickly through the documents and images, some old, some barely written, some only partly received into the collection. He feels he has gleaned for the Display what will most convince, most move Stella on behalf of what he imagines to be the wishes of Ada, as abstruse and contradictory as he knows those wishes to be.

Maps and Plans

Looking out from his workshop on Luna, Marty closes his eyes and pictures *Ultravioleta* fully formed. Marty approaches the great ships as both builder and sailor. He records his commentary as he works. Occasionally he stops fashioning thick sheets of paper into the massive craft and puts words on them.

"The paper ship dominates our age," he notes. "It is the nature of the ship to float and tear and turn like a page. A certain formality obtains on these vessels. Once elaborated, they are able to anticipate the dangers of the enhanced relaxation required in thought travel. The vicissitudes of associative movement through imagined space are survivable only as a result of the collaboration of beings who doubt each other's existence while depending on each other for their livelihoods. Group travel by this kind of consensus is so dangerous as to be considered impossible by some and by others not to be happening even while it is occurring.

"Brain cell meets paper airplane," Marty mutters to himself. "*Ultravioleta*," he whispers in I as he applies himself to the mainmast. Marty straddles a column of thick almost viscous material. The paper of the paper ships is resilient. It is elastic, flawed, porous and is incredibly absorbent of human detritus, mental or physical. Marty's particular refinement is to include personal correspondence in the mix. The added distance available from such an innovation is as great as the corollary danger of foundering by sheer excess of emotional content.

"Where there is paper," Marty thinks hungrily, "there is human passion and trouble. There is thinking and travel. There is time." Tiny thoughtful ships inundate Marty's revery but when he works he has only one ship in mind.

"*Ultravioleta.* Boat of being, Titanic of time," he hums. "Bigger and better. Thick with letters. Note of seeing. You are alive," he sings, "and you are mine."

Swiftly, Marty assembles the ship. Picturing the strings of the ancient guitar from his other life, he threads the lowest sheets of something like a wing or a sail to the mast. The ambiguity inherent in constructing a ship for thought travel is given, the trick is to maintain a symbolic amplitude while providing for the expected guest services such as hamburgers and radio.

Marty's experience with materials, the result of his occupation of the life of artist Xavier Martinez as well as the sheer bad luck of his acquaintance with Pontius, have made him the inevitable choice for the position of shipbuilder and navigator of *Ultravioleta.* Marty's knack for being in the wrong place at the wrong time first became evident as he crawled out the window of his collapsed studio in San Francisco, October 19, 1906. Marty remembers it well. Getting himself from one place to the other quickly, surviving, transcending, defenestrating, being both foreign and local, alien and alienated, retaining the craft of his father's bookbinding business in Guadalajara and adding to it his own decades long practice as a painter and draughtsman are qualifications so profound as to enter themselves like pages into the *Ultravioleta*'s log before she even launches. Marty consolidates. He teaches and sails. He prevails.

"I am me," he continues to work and sing. "*Ultra V* is me. Going out in her is my destiny."

"Martinez!" Pontius enters face first like a snake from one of the partly constructed voids Marty is trying to mold into a porthole.

"Demon from hell," Marty mumbles around his cheroot, adding, "No one calls me that."

"Funny, everyone calls me that. I am good and I can see you are yourself as ever. Just wanted to check on our little project. I don't mean to interfere with your process here but I wanted to remind you and to introduce a few concepts that I felt would be good to incorporate. So I will just reel off some of the usual iterations." Pontius closes in, violating Marty's personal space as he does with everyone. Even his fellow monsters attempt to give Pontius a wide berth. "The basic concepts," he goes on, "like dynamo, dilettante, Dante, demo – are you getting these? Denial, demon – ha! as you said. Let me see...denizen, deep, detritus, venison, denizen, skin, scan...You know it's a long trip and we don't want to..."

"Go away," Marty doesn't look up, though their I hearts mingle, as if a third eye or second mouth were always open on each of them. Marty blows violet smoke from his nose. It curls thickly up toward the dome of the old rocket hangar in the ruins of Tranquility Base V. He likes to call this hostile place his thinking chamber and generally welcomes all visitors. He retains the gregariousness of his former life, but Pontius always take up more space than there is. Marty looks up finally, fingering the red silk of the scarf draped around his neck like a noose.

"*Vamos*," he tries.

"We don't want to run out of steam, so to speak. I mean not to say…"

"But you do say, if I do say so myself you say and say again. You are without end, my friend."

Marty climbs up to the deck he has been fashioning. Scaling himself down to a punctuation point on its vast page, he works to establish a route where the mind's eye can travel through and around the vessel. He stitches and states and stretches the point, almost managing to undo Pontius' sentences before he has a chance to utter them, but not quite managing.

"We have a schedule, man. I've got a whole potful of humans arriving. Some of them think they are here already. They expect me to…." He wants to say take care of them but can't quite say it. "I am the government around here you know. I need to put them on the boat."

Marty knows that *Ultravioleta* is incomplete but believes he can see the end of it in his head.

"Just a matter of going through the motions," he says, trying to put Pontius off. Like every other contractor who has undernegotiated his deal, Marty is an optimist. "I'll just make the thing space worthy so we can get her past Mars. That's the thing. Don't want to get stuck in that Martian rut — sucked down into the ersatz world and their ersatz war."

"Ah yes, Mars," Pontius rolls the word like candy on his big tongue.

He pictures the pilots and captains of time standing at their bridges and on their decks, old maps of Mars spread out before them irresistible in the new vellum. Paper like that can take you anywhere. Mars can seem like an open book. You float by and you are hooked.

"Maybe we should stop," Pontius muses aloud. "See a little action on the way to the library. We'll have something to write home about." He smiles.

"We can't do it. *Ultravioleta* is not a battleship."

"You know that isn't true. Any ship within range can join in the battle there. It is hard to stay away. There is no question of the difficulty of attacking Mars." Pontius warms to the idea. "Everyone attacks Mars. It is just a question of being there and wanting to attack. That world was made for war or of war. The old Utopian Mars — distasteful idea that it was — is happily long lost. It is so far gone out of memory as to seem never to be have been real."

Marty sees Mars in Pontius' mind, unfolded on a table like a diagram of a crystal or chrysalis, laid out in dangerous symmetry. He knows that this Mars is like fate. "It is the bait you want not to take," he says more to himself than to Pontius. "The very mention of the red world is enough to distract anyone from all thoughts of construction, construction of thoughts," he warns. "If only you can get to it, you can get out of it — get it to you —

Wait! How does that go?" Marty goes on, attempting to invoke the Gutenberg library jingle to focus Pontius on what awaits them there, though he suspects it will only cause him to circle back to his tiresome lists of cargo text.

"Luckily," Marty reflects, "I am a professional." He begins to work, ignoring Pontius. He delights in the mental flight of this work. He sails before himself, damning the torpedoes.

Observing that Marty is moving in the right direction, Pontius slides out. He hovers, big and gelatinous. He relocates his scattered passengers wandering through the malls of the moon. He readies himself for the journey, collecting and recollecting his thoughts. He reloads.

Because the Sun

"Our conversation, and by this I mean yours with the government and mine with eternity, has never really left off." Wyatt enters Stella's mind by force.

Naked on paper, in her paper ship. Stella travels light. Bright. Wyatt's statement is in her head. It can't be shaken off but she shakes her head as if to rid herself of it, of him. Her long hair is light. She is made of light. "I am just another blonde," she thinks, "except for this map on my face."

Stella keys in her words, instead of speaking into the machine. She hates speech. The I haunt speech. They can't stay out of your head, but Stella is isolate in her being. When she thinks she takes up the space they have taken. She takes it back, stares into their eyes even when they are not present and have no eyes. But are they ever present? No one knows. She doesn't know. She knows only that she is grateful for the weightlessness of this chamber. She is finally able to think here in the unease of what she knows to be her natural state. *Nautilus*. Not. Nothing holding her down or together. Nothing back. She is alone in her ship. Compartmentalized, invested, invaded. In the context of stars — stellar. Like a banner of herself.

Isti Mirant Stella

"Though our past contact did not result in an agreement, there were results," Wyatt continues in her head, entering her thought-stream, a stanza away but closing. He flies to her in a little vessel

89

he lovingly and perhaps with some irony calls the *Stella*. He doesn't explain himself. He doesn't name the results. Stella thinks she knows them. "We can surely use what we learned to go forward. Go into the future. Or exist together in the same place at the same..."

"Where will we be when we go? And when will we go?" she interrupts. "I have fought with you and died for you. Of you. Several times. You have never told a lie I didn't believe. Or should I ask how far you are willing..."

"You were not alone on that planet. You were not the only one who died. I have been driven by desire," he claims, "to trust that you will turn again. My war is..."

"Your persuasion, like that war," she cuts in, "is always in the past with me, as you know. My capitulation is assumed. It is your attention that wanders. You go off. You have gone. The timing is wrong. It's a physical thing. Our side dies — really dies — because that is what we do and it's not like it is for you. And then we must begin again. And it seems that beginning is what you are about and you plan to continue to begin...if replacement is simply..."

Stella floats away. They are in two places at the same time. Two ships. Her gilded craft is caught in an arc – the solar system trails behind. The *Stella* like a kite soars in the nothing of space and time. They remember the battles. The silent explosions. The silence. They remember their own battles, also silent.

"If it is addiction, it is like ours to air," she thinks, thinking, "Even my thoughts are not my own." She makes them so with a determined effort of veiling. Wyatt feels it. "This death in life. The presence of the threat. I don't want it," she says to herself, feeling his penetration of her thought, "but it's the only thing I want. The discontinuity we make makes what we call the world seem as desirable as it is false."

"My sense," she goes on, "is that your life, my life, my living at all, is less important to you than your desire to take up where we left off…to build this trust…and yet you allow for something, anything, to happen that will change history. You come on like some sort of omen flaming over us. Over me. But I am omen not you. I won't read you that way. We can't go back there. We shouldn't want to. One of us doesn't. One of us just wants to go on. Into nothing."

"But what is your question?" Wyatt falls back on his usual device. "Your objection?"

"If by question you mean pleasure. You know what the answer is but not what it will do, though you should know, as it is clear what it has done. What you have done. It is possible that I seek nothing," she goes on, "that you only imagine that what I want to know is what you want to tell me. That I am formed to you."

Wyatt experiences her "Formed to you" as observation and complaint, as objection. They know together it is the complaint of anyone against the I. There is much they know together but Wyatt knows there is missing information. That they resist each other is something they have in common but it is also, again, the past, though fresh in both their minds, as they both know. A sense of interim vexes their exchange, as if a thousand years interrupts each word, spoken or written. Thought is unacknowledged between them, it is what they do, what they have done. Or so

Stella believes. True to himself, Wyatt is not saying what he could say. He has a card he is not playing.

"I am perhaps not who you think I am," Stella maintains but Wyatt objects.

"You Marys are all alike. When will you admit that you are not dead. I have not killed you or remembered you into death. I am not Petrarch and you are not Laura. This isn't that world. This isn't the world at all."

"But people have died. I have died over and over... You have killed me..."

"How can you even think you could be in that danger again?" he demands. She sees him in her mind's eye, reaching for the knife. "The quality of your attention would not allow you to be vulnerable."

"I was thinking of the form of the sonnet not of being one of its victims," she counters. "Your little songs. Little suns. We can make one again."

It is her best offer. They know it together. Wyatt is fully Wyatt now. Fully I. He remembers the last ride on his last horse. His face grows bony and dark in its sleek beard like an animal. His white shirt is open at the throat. His look is black. He considers her risk. He wonders if he can kill her again or get her back. He considers the form they are about to fill.

"Because the sun," he begins

"Here without us or within
This room" she continues, "porthole
Stage or frame or window"
"I can't go into," she writes "or past"
"Our past," writing over her, "matters
Less" She flies into the sun "than what
Now might" "Please don't" Turning. Forcing her to turn. "We talk
Among" "The edge of it is too much. It is too
Strong because the light is" "Us as you
Defined as not, and this wrongly,
As me" Stella insistent and still again now flying low
"Giving in means leaving off as oneself dying" He crosses her
"Into you. Not being left" He responds "As I am not"

Pulling away again she pulls away, knowing she won't be followed.
He never follows in a physical sense. She is sure what she thinks
about it. She has won. She wins every time she doesn't die.

"Why not win?" she dreams as she flies. "Why not collaborate?
Report back. Maybe there is a government. Tell them everything.
Survive. Pretend to be alive. Continue."

Daily Epitaph

On his way, Wyatt again, Virgil Wyatt Earp. Like any spurned lover he goes to his other life, his other wife. He hums his song. Long may his story echo like the blank destiny of the unsigned check. One life ago and the tune stays in his head. The name stays. The identity remains coded not in the story but in the statement. The balance. How much is taken? How much given? To have the chance to go down hard. The Spicer Decision. By the existence of the sentence or lack thereof, Wyatt is driven into his other name.

"…standing their ground and fighting back — giving & taking death with unflinching bravery."

"There are paths," Wyatt writes as himself, looking into the future of the life that seems to be burning out from under him like a sinking ship. "They intersect in the past. There is a lot of space. But we are not alone in it. The dance of the fight is misrepresented, misremembered by the duelists. It is the focus of the inquiry. The exoneration is a matter of law. I am not in the tower now but in the street. *Quickness to begin this tragedy.* Innocence is sweet with me here. The badge is mine. The dirt in the very street will be owned by me. There are brothers on both sides. They (I) lie as they hit the ground and die face down. The light from that remembered world is my light now. Silver in patterns in lines already lost. Pattern overlaid on a pattern. A desert ago. A civilization in love with death."

The lullaby of this condition is a refrain Wyatt finds suits his alienated mind.

"The song has a reason for being," he continues, the blue ink seems oceanic on the deserted page. "Like me, as I, Wyatt, not but yes am saloon keeper and sometime sheriff. I make this statement as my epigraph, my epitaph. Deputized earlier and later detective. In my official and infinite capacity," he goes on. "We were strong," he hums like the radio. "No one can tell us we're wrong."

Lit against the sun, Wyatt remembers the reward. He remembers Ike's story, telling it to himself like a miser counting his money.

"Clanton. Known to some for his felonius anxiety. Then and now." Wyatt alters his voice, speaking in I. "Wanted and then wanted poster. That I would be tempted by. Dead or alive. Check on the order. That he was and then they sent a telegram soon after telling everything. They spoke of Ike. How he died in front of the Alhambra in Tombstone in 1881. It has just begun. I read and showed the writ. I wrote it. I made my entrance. I entered his heart with thought and then with metal. The bells rang for the boys that day.

"As quick as thought and certain as death…we made use of our official capacity as a pretext for blasting every Clanton out of town and off the planet. Virgil and I. We were known and well-known as leaders of men, as takers of life and thought, as defenders of what was right for us. Witnesses of credibility who stood up behind and before us and claimed controlling importance. They counted. The dead had resisted arrest. They fired before they were shot. Who shot first? It doesn't matter. They brought matters on themselves. They claimed, insulting 'We are not ready to leave town just yet.' But they did go.

"The Spicer Decision was decided then. It is on record that we were innocent of the crime. In view of the past history of the county and the generally believed existence at this time of desperate, reckless men in our midst banded together and living by predation, regarding neither life nor property in their career and to parade the streets armed with repeating [rifles] and six-shooters is both monstrous and startling. This was said by the deceased before he got that way and that is another story of the future but looking back you see only the shooting and I survived."

Wyatt reflects, quiet now, at his desk which he mans like a pilot. He writes of his rights. He claims them.

"It was this speaking and belief about the street and its quality of life that brought about the time which ended. I was there. The OK Corral was not a corral but the back door of a barn. Based more on the implications of position and character than with the facts of the incident, the Spicer Decision canonized the Earps, especially myself, along with Doc Holliday. We set the stage for books, daguerreotypes, appearances and consultancy in Hollywood. Doc was doomed from the start but the event allows him to presurvive his death.

"They flee from the melee, who were mingled up in it. The arrest comes and something turns on arrested motion, as oneself to oneself. Doc is deliberate, bless him, he is quick but slow. A series of statements makes the flight inevitable in the fight. The replay shows it all. Declaration of the Clantons: 'Shoot them on sight.' An earlier deal and blow to the head. The latter struck by the former.

Virgil being chief of police at this time crushed the law-defying element. Bad, desperate, reckless creatures, that was us. We are I."

Wyatt relaxes into the hopelessness of resisting that fate lived over again. The death of his friend and lover is like every other death. Only his own, because it seems impossible and yet completely likely, even inevitable, has any interest for him.

"The trial was more perfect than the event. We prevail, proving ourselves in every detail righteous. For me it is always the beginning of a new life of celebrity and celebration, acceleration. The earliest version is true because that's how it was. We won. I won. The bells rang. The boys died. Not unlike life after all. One's thought is the only frontier between life and death. The explosion inside goes everywhere.

"On a steel horse I ride," Wyatt hums, getting back to himself.

"We are wounded. We don't die. *Corpus delicti*. I was delectable to me, to us. William Clanton fell or was shot at first fire. Thomas McLaury was unarmed but for the Winchester rifle on the horse beside him. William Clanton and Frank McLaury met the demand for surrender by drawing their pistols. Witnesses at a distance and those mingled up or fleeing from the melee came to say. The legend was later. We made it stick at fairs, demonstrations and circuses. The Hollywood connection was sweet. My wife Josephine — Jessie — that was later. I got her with my reputation. Later there was the bio. *My Wyatt*. The work of it she did on the California edge of the Great Basin. Desert streets. Bakersfield.

"You don't know me, but you don't like me." Wyatt winds down, preparing to head back into his other life.

"All I can say of it is that it was no dream. One Wyatt for the other and a life away. First for last," Holliday responds quietly. "Morgan like the witch. Virgil your brother and guide, my guide. I am your known associate. A.K.A. Doc. We put ourselves inside each other's minds. Gambler, barfly, dentist. That was me, dying anyway. That same crowd at the bar. Jessie belongs to another man. You take her. The three of us live it up and then down, as far as we can go down."

"It was the main chance, the one we had to take," Wyatt says. It is as if he is already gone. "To have gone out — you and I — like me and Stella. It's the money minute — when it all opens up. But you have to pay. Everyone pays the official. That is always me. The official statement. 'I am an official of the town.' I am this place, this corral. It is from me that people flee. O.K. G.I. No talk. Bang. Bang. They are gone. That sometime did me seek."

Wyatt rises. Holliday takes his hand and retains it for a moment as Wyatt pulls away. Words echo in Doc's head, but he is silent as he watches the doors of the bar swing closed.

"He saves the ones He wants to save."

Maryolatry

"Dazed in silent explosions. Pasted down in fragments. We are strangely bent. Something like a smile or an eye hovers or opens. Wings spread like a new belief. Who are these monsters?" Ada writes at her table. She is expecting her assistant Dayv but can't remember having met him. "Things are occurring out of sequence," she thinks. "If it's a time storm we are deeply fucked. But of course I can't know that, though I think I do know it." She resumes her work on the war. As usual she writes and collects images — sometimes of herself but mostly not. She doesn't always know.

She feels herself running though she is writing. The panic and dust are there again like the sweet airless poison that is the Martian atmosphere.

Ada makes it across a street where Stella lies prone.

Two hundred million guns rage in an oddly quiet battle. Huge clouds inappropriate and terrific rise up. There are no clouds on Mars.

Ada coils around Stella, gives her air. They enter into an earnest discussion about breath and death. "In," Ada mutters, "Baby. Out. There's something going on here."

She bends over Stella. "But if you could just breathe for me," she gives her air again, "I could maybe figure it or maybe it doesn't figure," and again, "Just don't die on me," cradling her as Stella seems to wake. "There's nowhere to go, but we really have to go."

Martians in rows behind fall down one by one. Everyone plays a part in the war. Ada finds them. Their pictures and statistics. She finds them and counts them. "There are many kinds of Martian but one kind of war," she writes. "Things explode for no reason or for reasons of their own. The dead are all soldiers once they have died. The world is littered with them. An incursion occurs or has occurred of light into a dark place. Too much light. Beams or rays razor-like go through everything. There is a lack of air in the screams. A lack of conviction in the eyes of the victims as they turn red or blue or gray depending on the weapon and on the speciation."

Ada and Stella hide in their tiny corner. They turn into each other. Like a play within a play they struggle to be separate from the drama going on around them. Finally they run. Flat out. They run away.

Running again as writing. Is she in life or only remembering it. "Perhaps I died there." Ada doesn't know. It is like any other night on Mars. Dust and things vaporized. Never enough air. A clash of realities of the worst type. No quarter offered by the believers. None expected by the targets. Women and clones fight the war. Fought the war. They seem to fight over and over. They think they are heading out, that they have gone, but ultimately they find what they fear. They are headed back, back into the war, into a planetary context of conflict and despair. There is nothing that is not unreal there. Only dislocation. Something takes you, draws you back and grinds you down, poured like ashes over the battlefield. Once empty. Now full again.

An overflight of Marys, called from all over the system, approaches. Most are shocked to find themselves back. Some have never been to Mars. That they are Marys was only recently discovered to them by an ability to travel by thought and by a compulsion to fight in a war that most humans gave up in advance and any clone knows is hopeless.

Ada wrestles with it. Her work on the war is as much a struggle for her as her relationship with Stella. They contend in every way. Ada and Stella. Ada and the war. Physical, mental, emotional. Never really meeting but always in pursuit, as anyone was with Stella.

"She does follow me at times when I go. She does come. Not often but it's a sight to see."

Ada tries to find her place with Stella or in time. But she can't find it and they can't agree on the war. Whether there is a point to it. Their conversations are intricate and frustrating.

"That the war was fought for the Information Imperatives seems unlikely enough," Stella begins.

"And yet it was. It is," Ada counters. "Either it is absurd to fight a war over representing or there is no other reason to fight. I have said it before. The fundamental right of anyone not to actually become information, not to be productized, traded, copied, sold, sold to, sold out — the right to be real and live in a real world is something like what the Imperatives were about. You know that."

"I don't know it and neither do you. No one has ever read these

Imperatives. Nothing is real anyway, least of all some imaginary clonish manifesto about Martian sales trends. Who cares?"

"The versions of them proliferated. They were inaccurate and in doubt." Ada retells the story. "They were never written down or conveyed in electronic form. In a way that was the point. They were inexact, unreproducible, designed only to resist that Mars Utopia thing everyone comes here for. They see it fail but they never stop believing in it. And who are we to tell them otherwise. Just some hyperdesigned clone like me and then you — female overstock brought here for the men. Naturally we don't believe in their idealism. We aren't designed to. We're designed for them, except in my case. I am designed for you."

"You're not. You are just the past in the form of flesh, Mama. Mistress of the Byron hotel library chain. Born to check us in and check us out. To keep track. All this counting. If you could count backward and cancel yourself I think you would."

"Not alone though. I'd want to cancel you too."

"No." Stella is not going along with anything. "No one cancels me. And nobody brought me here. Nobody brings me anywhere." She is already looking for a way out.

"Well then baby you are my Utopia. I admit it. But that means two things. It means you are my problem, my dream. And it means you don't exist."

Ada struggles with Stella. She struggles with time. She seems to remember the conversation as she is having it. She tries to write and see the events, to arrange them. But Martian history is active.

It is interactive. As she writes she is in the fight, to save Stella, to escape, repeatedly, to come back.

The Marys hover and leave. They hover and crash or drop their bombs. Information floats obscuring and yet magnifying the battlefield like some sort of electronic gas. The fiery explosions produced by the government are so much background to the real show. Events are interpreted as or before they happen. Mary bombs are made of facts. But the accuracy of the information in these bombs isn't legible to the targets or readers. They become confused once they are hit or die, as with any other bomb.

"That the heroics of the flyovers make up for the deaths is questionable," Ada writes. "The whole idea of women and clones is a misnomer. It hides the men and the I who died. Or at least the men. The war fought along gender lines to end such lines and other illusions ended nothing."

"Nothing ends," she says to Dayv who looks unconcerned and at home in this endlessly retold, refought, pointless and hopeless war.

"It is my war," he says to himself. "But wait — did the I cause it? Or even possibly did I cause it? Are they even here other than occasionally as pilots. Is Mars their idea? Our idea? Is it a trick? What about sex?" he warms to his subject. "Did the I divide us or were there always sexes?" Dayv wonders disingenuously. Of course he knows it was the I. Everything is them. As a child of an I he should know. As a human he remembers. He looks into Ada's eyes for an answer or corroboration but he sees only the war. He sees her on Mars with Stella though he sits with her in the library orbiting Europa. He regards the woman he thinks of as his boss and the one who he believes to be his mother with something like reverence and nostalgia. They are caught. Everyone on Mars is caught. He feels the Marys swarm Parphar and his worldview widens. He emerges from this long revery onto a street in the city. Ada and Stella run and at the same time arrive beside him, in separate ships, as Marys.

Ada writes at her table. Simultaneously she sees herself and Stella fall from the Martian sky into certain death. At the library again, dazed, she looks up at Dayv who waits for her to tell him what to do, but she doesn't know what he should do. She looks down into Stella's vivid eyes.

Ada, Stella and Dayv think together for a moment, steadfastly, in the library. They feel themselves to be at Ada's table, sitting together. Dayv rolls tiny Martian cigarettes for something to do. They smoke. The paper burns their hands helpfully, making them believe they are where they are. They lay their heads on their folded arms. Stella senses something about Dayv. She believes it has to do with his work at the library. He looks familiar.

"Are you a clone?" she tries to ask, but they have all fallen asleep.

The horizon blows up repeatedly. The explosions are stiff. They seem to take a long time to happen. Stella and Ada look around to see if they have died. They look at each other and down at themselves. Dayv watches with his usual calm. They put their hands flat on the table, closing their eyes, imagining a ring of safety. As if this could work.

"As we sleep we fly and as flying die back into sleep," Ada writes later, if it is later. "The mixture of times in the Martian landscape is hideous and exhausting. The idea of a time storm doesn't begin to describe it. People die over and over. Weapons blaze and melt away. There is no end to the war. Each combatant eventually realizes it is the same war, tries to escape, lives in the future and is drawn back down. The Maryolatry is reduced to a slogan. Women and clones – though we were never the only ones. But maybe we were," she continues. "Maybe we are. Identifying with these despised creatures justifies nothing. Things used to happen once. There was a history. Everyone claims it. Now there is only repetition."

As a hybrid, Dayv has a unique perspective, but he doesn't care. As I he wants to eat. And as I he realizes he is always eating. It is the beautiful thing about being one of the boys. They are not really all boys. But they are always eating. As human Dayv wants to be in the library. He believes there is someone he should meet. Some bit of organizational culture he should share but the war rises back up in his mind as soon as he seems to get there. Dayv looks into the middle distance seeing the endless battle beyond his eyes. Ada writes. She watches. She finds two women struggling to survive. She sees Stella. She sees herself as someone else. She writes as if against gravity, knowing herself to be running and falling and flying.

"Bombs light up the sky. The streets of Parphar are like day though it is night and later like night though day. A woman runs through the streets with unnatural speed. She finds air where there is none. She finds a woman. She sees her fall."

The Wind Screams Mary

All around Ada at the café, people live their dreams. Martians are attached like marsupials to their barstools, respirators hanging on and off their ragged faces. They drink and breathe and talk as they take their ease from the war. Ada twists around in her stool, facing the courtyard and little sea of tables. Why she is here again in Parphar she doesn't know, anymore than she ever knew why she was on Mars. She turns back to the bar, feeling herself expect someone. She figures it is Stella. Ada sips her tea. Maskless and self-contained, she takes in the thin air, and basks in the cool light of the tiny sun.

The red dusk emphasizes the red plant light and the rose of the thermal dome, miles overhead, intact for once. The walls and tea are green. The wood of the bar is dark blonde like Stella. Ada closes her eyes into the waves of enhanced caffeine. She feels rather than sees Stella at the threshold, feels the gravity of her disturb the air as she approaches and comes to rest by her side. Stella leans slightly into Ada's space. The bartender drifts over, pours tea into a new cup and seems gone before he has arrived. Ada and Stella look up at where he was.

"Stell." Ada closes her eyes though they are already closed. Stella stares into her cup in what is for her an odd moment of complete joy.

"I love tea," she says finally.

"You seem better. Not that you are. I don't think we can ever be better, but you feel as though…you are…"

"Yeah. Clear. Things are clear." Stella breathes deeply but quietly, economically, barely using the device. There is a gold down on her arms. It looks yellow in the red light.

"You are back."

"I am back but am going out also. I am not really here. I don't know why I seem here when I should be there. I am going all the way out, past where you are. Past the library. I'll stop by."

Ada looks fully at Stella for the first time.

"You are coming to me?"

"I am stopping by."

"Good."

"I can't not be here now. I couldn't not come back. I hate this war."

"It suits you, this blue stuff." Ada takes the measure of Stella's transparency, her gaze directing the eyes of other patrons, an I or two hones in, already distracted by Stella, who twists, stretching herself in her barstool, creating the ripple of attention only she could make in a stunned, hyper-caffeinated crowd like this one, nodding in and out of time, in some cases barely alive. The hard quality of a pilot in full flight shimmers off her, though she is also just a blonde in a bar.

They hold hands in silence, missing each other already though they are not yet gone. Stella bleeds to death in Ada's arms in memory or sometimes Ada saves her. Sometimes she cannot be saved. The war goes on and on.

"Take care of yourself, baby. You owe me that."

"I don't owe you shit." Stella whispers. She walks away.

Time stops for Ada. She becomes unsure of her location, closing her eyes against knowing where she is, hoping to find herself back at the library.

"Derangement of both time and place," she thinks wearily as she wanders through the tables. When she finally sees Eddie Zed she feels relieved and surprised though nearly everyone on the planet knows he is always right where she is seeing him now, doing what he is doing, which, she thinks, making her way to him, is probably writing to herself.

"Hello, sailor," she says meeting the heat in his cold eyes with her own warmth. "Got a light?"

Legend of Blood

On Mars though not of it, more of an alien than the creatures he despises, Eddie is alone as always. He allows for Ada's approach with what is for him unusual openness. She sits down at his table where she knows no one ever sits, carefully not reacting to the change she perceives in him. She chooses also not to react to Pontius who she recognizes behind Eddie, transparent, looming, voracious.

"I'm not sure why I try," she begins, looking away from Pontius, using her own predicament, well known between them, as a way of not referring to Eddie's awful state. "I can't forget. I can't not go to her — even if I am not really here in this time or place. Or anywhere."

"We never forget anything," Eddie rasps, not looking up from his work. "We can't."

As he speaks, Eddie breathes shallowly into his mask and continues to write in his notebook. He seems to write what he says as he says it, crossing out passages and writing them again. It occurs to Ada, not for the first time, that it is as bad to be a Martian as to be a clone. Eddie, she also notes, is still beautiful, and yet there is something strange about him, a blurring, as if he were being badly transmitted. She knows it is because of Pontius but doesn't bother to say anything. Eddie registers her thoughts with his eyes, also not bothering to reply in words, though he speaks constantly.

"Without rereading the book, without rewriting it, how can we know we exist?" he says.

Ada watches as Eddie reads himself, noting that the charismatic impact, the sheer magnetism that is his particular quality, has not changed with this blurring — is, if anything, stronger. His thick dark hair is the same. He has those same eyes like heaven. His perfectly formed hands, smooth against the rough paper, veined like the marble of the table, seem almost translucent as he lays his pen aside and rests them against his teacup.

Pontius throbs quietly behind him.

"They say I write in blood," he goes on, beginning to write again, though he also continues to look at Ada. "That the page is my territory, my space, my container. Or maybe I say it. Maybe I say that my veins hollow out like avenues through this city where I am marooned. Let's say this is Parphar, since it is. Let's say it's the ruins of Parphar. I am here but I dream it nonetheless. I dream my streets. The courtyard of the café is a vast construction like a memory palace. I dream it and say it. We say it."

The marble table feels cool to Ada. "Like a human tomb," she thinks.

She watches as Eddie blurs again. The air around them seems to lack air. Like the other Martians, Eddie breathes with an apparatus. He feels he is a mechanism. He takes a breath of mechanical air. Watching him, Ada realizes she has forgotten to breathe. Her mask hangs uselessly away from her face. She wonders why Stella is never not in her mind, while breathing is something she can't quite remember to do. Ada tries to think about breathing, but finds she can't think of it.

"What is it called?" she asks Eddie, looking at his notebook, trying to get something else into her head.

"*The Astrologer*," he answers, relieved. Eddie needs to speak as much as Ada needs to listen. He closes his eyes, mentally entering the book spread out before him in a manuscript blackly elaborated with changes and additions.

"The title has the advantage of seeming to refer to myself. As you know, I am not a believer in the mantic sciences, but I have occasionally found them useful. My work refers indirectly to the various necromancies associated with this planet — to the mad structures imposed on it by the many monsters of Mars. Like yourself, I work for the victims, though it is the monsters who interest me. I want to speak to the idea that someone or something, whether scientist or pseudoscientist, could organize or control or at least foretell their depredations."

"But who are they?" Ada encourages him.

"You know who they are. They are the phantoms — politicians, wolfmen, vampires, generals, governors, like the Roman, Pontius Pilate — my special friend, as you see — the usual demons conjured up by Martians or recorded by us, as if an image could prove anything. To me, the I are just another threat. Only Pontius, who seeks me out, who in fact dogs me constantly — only Pontius is generative. He is *my* monster. I see him as the pure symbol of the bureaucratic, governmental betrayal endemic to Mars."

Ada sees it now — that Eddie craves Pontius' attention as much as Pontius seeks him out. She discerns again the heavy imperial shadow of the ancient I she knows so well. She thinks of him as a devil's devil. She wonders why he appears to be in so many places at once. She knows she knows but can't bear the implications of her knowledge. Pontius' intense regard enters her as she thinks of him. Quickly closing herself off, she looks to Eddie, who continues to speak in his airless voice.

"There is a quality in Pontius that makes him a collector of that which is human and alive and full of blood. He looks for real physical sacrifice, to himself if possible but, again, it is the blood he wants, as if it was for the empire he no longer represents. The pain and redness of my book — the redness of the blood — excite him. It excites them. The I. They want to be read — to be red. He has chosen to be a predator. He is the foil to all of the human vulnerability that remains anywhere, especially in me. Whatever, whoever else he is doing, he is stalking me."

At first this seems inaccurate to Ada, but then she realizes it is simply true.

"Pontius is the perfect monster," she says. "Perfect for you."

"Exactly," Eddie agrees. "You can see the use of such an imperial enemy to me in my identity as Stendahl."

"You can't escape?" she says, thinking of the endless wanderings of his namesake, but then she realizes the absurdity of asking this question of a Martian.

"I can't shake him and I can't keep him all the way out. It's worse than being in love. We are each other's subjectivity. It's like any I mind fuck except that it's not. It's never resolved because I do keep him out — mostly. I know the resistance is what he thrives on but

I can't stop and let him inside of me. I would kill him if he could die."

"As would we all," Ada says, though they both know how few outside of Mars even notice they are invaded.

"Here we hate everyone," Eddie comments proudly, in response to her thought.

"How is he different from just another of the Martian demons?" she asks, knowing but wanting to hear what he will say.

"He feels more like a local poet than a legendary monster, really," Eddie replies. "In a sense, he is the Astrologer as much as I am."

"So he is in the book?"

"The book is where he is in me, when I can keep him there," Eddie agrees. "Everything about the book is right for him. *The Astrologer* is not a work of interpretation or one of original scholarship or fiction, though in places it is a story and it is demonstrably false. He fits into the book like a maggot on a corpse. Though he is superficial and temporary, it is through him that the legends make themselves felt. Their implications become apparent as I think through them, through him, to produce the text. At times it is about him, in some way, or at times it is unrelated," Eddie goes on, "except by blood," he adds.

"So the monster stands in for his victims?" Ada asks, watching Eddie grow more animated and yet also very still.

"Precisely. Pontius exhibits the unchanging yet cyclical nature of my subjects, their culture, their place in history, their lack of it. Each of my words takes us both farther into them, burrowing in a spiral trajectory I hope will bring me back out again, though I suspect it will not."

"So you invade him?"

"Oh yeah," Eddie's dark eyes get darker. "Whenever, wherever."

"And the Countess?" Ada refers to the other character in Eddie's book.

"She is you in a way, but really she is more Stella — though it is only through you that I know her."

Eddie grows silent as he considers his story, as if taken up by it again. Using one of his immaculate hands to hold open the note-book, he writes with the other in a close script, but then stops, closing his eyes as if in pain. He brings a hand to his head as if try-ing to discern a barely heard sound. The tips of his fingers press against his temples, closing around his forehead until his head is balanced in his hands like a globe on a stand. He rocks slightly from side to side, looking absently out over the café tables at the other Martians. They are silent except for the rasp of their appa-ratus. It is true that if they spoke he wouldn't really hear them. He hears only Ada and the drone of his own thoughts. Eddie and the Martians breathe together, but he is separate from them.

"As you know, the I, like vampires, are said not to breathe except cosmetically. That this is untrue is less interesting to me than that it is said. Entities who are said, accurately or otherwise, not to die — that's where it is for me. Are the I immortal or do they simply die offstage? Or, as everyone says, do they have the ability to make one forget their deaths, to forget mortality at all, including one's own? I believe that they die. I hate them — though I know it is what they want from me – what Pontius wants — the distress, the obsession, the temporary closeness of predator and prey. Pontius is ready for any part in the discussion, to speak is to eat for him. We are alike there. If anything about him is legendary it is that. Even among the always hungry, he is known for his appetite. Like me he wants to get back to the blood, the stories of the blood. Like me, he loves the red planet legends told among the few actual Martians who have been here for generations. I use them as I use him to make and remake the stories. He has in common with us that the creature he inhabits comes from millenia of terrestrial despair."

"Only those with nothing to lose have ended up on Mars," Ada says. "As everyone knows. It is widely regarded as a curse to have been born here — or by Martians to have been born at all. That's why it is harder for the I on Mars and yet better. They are better."

Eddie peers at Ada with his unnaturally blue eyes. She goes on.

"There are others here who are said not to die, also Martians — also monsters. Can you die, Eddie? Beings who don't die can remember for a long time. They are made of memory. You are made of memory. You remember for me, and for them."

"Yes," Eddie responds quietly, looking down, continuing to balance his perfect head in his hands like a planet at the far edge of the galaxy. "The ankle deep blood of legend," he mutters, beginning to write again. Ada sees him experience the imperial crimes of the I over and over until tears are running down his face or, at least, he seems to cry.

"I can't love anything not human," he says to Ada and to the I in his mind, but he knows he can't love at all.

"If I had a heart it would long ago have succumbed to the breaking and tearing to which such organs are subject. I know this makes me less than human — like them. It makes me hate them all the more — those inhuman creatures who are my life's work."

Eddie looks up at Ada.

"At least I know I am essentially one of them. I am the apostatic remnant of catastrophe. I go on to the next thing, as episodic as any other demon."

"You are not a demon," Ada responds. She knows he expects her to defend him against himself. "And, not to be obvious, but what about the war?"

Ada sees that the war and time storms raging around Eddie are less real to him than the extremity of his own anguish or the lifeless damned who populate his work and his world. But she feels also that he should know finally that the shifts and paroxysms of daily life during the endless wars and his personal devastation are not unrelated. She wants to see him acknowledge the time storm.

"You see it, right?" she says. "Time should be constant here, or somewhere, but your one morning of writing, this continuous event at the café, has opened out into eons. Of course the legends are real. There is always a war to wake up to on Mars. The weapons alter thought and time. The Information Imperatives are ignored. Men and clones bleed. Women rain down like stones from an exploding sky."

"Yes, I know," Eddie speaks sadly but there is energy, even pleasure, in his anguish.

"The war has become part of *The Astrologer*, part of the story. The Astrologer is a magician, a con man, a sorcerer, a collaborator, a soldier in the time wars, as well as a monster. He casts the horoscope of time itself. He bends it to his will. He makes be what he wants to be by convincing, by reflecting back the desires of everyone. In the Countess, he has a companion, a twin, a victim. He is the observer of the hours, the horrors. He is drunk with what is possible when anything is possible. He is like me. He is pure fiction."

Eddie gazes into Ada's violet eyes, continuing as if mesmerized by her into the writing and speaking she would most wish to hear.

"I am just the plaything of the monsters," he complains, "I narrate. I contextualize and annotate. I develop and prove and show. I am a numbers man. I count the dead in my stories and in my mind. I keep track of the times when real Martians have died. As if there were real Martians in this war, or real death."

"I myself have…"

"Died?" Eddie continues. "I don't think so. Not like us. I have already not survived so many times that I know more about you than you know about yourself. Believe me when I tell you that you don't know your own mind. But you have helped me to know mine again. You always have."

"You record the faces and movements, the patterns of demise, as I do," Ada says, thinking that what he means to say is that their work with the victims is essentially the same. "They are the medium, they are the pattern beneath your story. The aesthetic and symbolic weaponry we use and describe reflects the continuing and endless rage of the victims, their silent cries."

Eddie holds his head again, nodding in what could either be agreement or intense pain or both.

"They are not silent," he says. "I hear them — always."

Pontius becomes more visible as Eddie fades. He continues to loom and feed. If someone else were as close to him as Eddie or as attentive as Ada, they would hear, as they do, his hideous laughter. They would see the tears of joy squeeze themselves out of his huge face.

Eddie lays his head finally on his manuscript as if it was a pillow. Believing he has fainted or fallen asleep, Ada realizes that she didn't know he could sleep. Seeing how deeply he sleeps, she seizes the opportunity to slide the manuscript out from under his perfect head, away from his immaculate grasp.

Previously she has read only the passages he has sent to the library but she knows the real work is in the changes, the handwritten elaborations, the marginalia, the lines and traces of his thought. Settling down to wait for him to wake, she begins to read.

The Astrologer: Prisoner of Mars

Rest among stars.

The face of the Countess rises above her starred silk bodice like Ganymede above Jupiter. The Astrologer attempts to explain the solar system to her. Tense but enervated, they lie together on a grassy patch of a nameless island in the Hourglass Sea. It is a sea of sand. They believe themselves to be captives here on Mars though, if asked, they would not be able to say why they are captured or where they were before.

In the Astrologer's explanation of the stars he refers to the sea of sand, but only in passing. In fact, his explanation is an argument or a plot. From the tone of it, the Countess perceives that there is something he wants from her. That he takes this tone, that of a lover's quarrel, in his argument is more mysterious to her than the stars themselves, though there have been times when she has had no trouble figuring it out. Time is not consistent on the island. It is one of the main problems of their captivity, the other being to figure out what the Astrologer could want. Mostly, as now, she feels as if she were created to ask herself the question of what he wants. She knows he is a fiction and that she herself is false. She hates knowing.

"Men like you," she says to herself, "what do they ever want?"

"But there are not," he looks up at her sweetly, "an infinite number of natural formations." They look out at the remnants of a garden. "In spite of what you might say about the stars."

The Countess and the Astrologer appear to rest together but they are not restful. The garden seems to decay before their eyes, the island where they are caught, to shrink, the sea of sand to turn to familiar Martian dust. In spite of all of this, the Astrologer contrives to lecture his companion.

"The plurality of systems," he goes on, "is understood to be effective or affective. The planets to represent in fact a system or determination of fortune as belonging to or being about…"

Troubled, the Countess looks at the Astrologer, unable to listen. In spite of the Martian winds, her elaborate coiffure retains its perfect form as she leans melodramatically into his space. Anyone but the Astrologer, seeing her now, would realize she is a construct, but the thought does not occur to him. He temporarily loses his place in his own thinking as she leans close but then he gets it again and opens his mouth to continue. She cocks her glossy head as if to hear him better.

"What are you saying?" she says.

"That the planets are our lives," he goes on, reaching for her.

"What are you doing?" the Countess asks. The Astrologer has taken her face in his hands to demonstrate the effect of the planets and the theory of the many worlds. Though she resists, she also makes a cooing sound.

"The worlds come to be…," he begins again.

"But what do you want?" she interrupts.

"The worlds come to be because they go around. They exist to revolve. The worlds are one within one of round things," he insists, making the point with his eyes as he peers into those of the Countess. He shapes his fingers into circles, holding them up to his eyes like spectacles. "They go round and round," he repeats.

The Countess sees what he means or in fact more than what he means to mean.

"Don't," she responds, but she takes his wrists into her own hands, making another circle. They both feel the circle as a gravitational field much like the one around the planet. But unlike Mars, which holds everything fast, the Countess is actually pushing the Astrologer away. And yet, like Mars and its prisoners, they remain connected, even as she disentangles herself from him. They make a theater of two in which the ancient winds of Mars are personified as themselves — along with the other natural phenomena whose measure it is the Astrologer's will to read. The Countess counts. Reacting to his ploy, she sings a repetitive a-tonal song.

What can this be?
We are not alive
Now or then
I ask again
Looking back at where you
From far off went
Saying you would end
Or know this
Your own head
Or had said
What you missed

That your mind is
Mine whatever I wish
To say or to have done
Now that you are gone
And are (not)
Officially
What I (don't)
Want

"There are monsters in the sky," he responds, though he knows she knows it. They wrestle weakly but determinedly again until the Countess relents and allows his head to fall into her lap where they both know it has never been before. The Countess looks down at him fondly but then she looks up and out at the endangered world around them.

The Astrologer and the Countess know together that they are out of place and out of time, that they are subject to an already completed fate, mere counters in a game being played in relation, but not in response to, their desires. They are aware of being characters in a script larger than the stories they tell themselves to pass the time. They know they are prisoners of Mars, prisoners also of the obsessive imaginings of their creator, Eddie Zed, in his identity as the writer Stendahl. As Stendahlian creatures in a hyperconscious universe alive with thought they know more than they want to know about their own context and yet they remain caught. The Astrologer believes he feels this more acutely than the Countess, but the Countess, though she is distracted by the polite but relentless assaults of the Astrologer, is exquisitely aware of the hopelessness of their situation.

The Astrologer falls asleep in the arms of the Countess, only to wake suddenly crying "*Annus mirabilis!*" referring to an old obsession, not his own, with life on Mars, but she knows it is a blind. He has another thing in mind. Something he wants done or wants to be done with.

"It is not about me. He is in love with his own life or wishes to be," the Countess reminds herself.

The Countess sees that the Astrologer wants to be done with the fiction of his extrapolation of life from lifeless stars. She knows that the wheel of fortune he imagines to be turning around him is made of the constellations of human events in time rather than events in the heartless atoms of the cosmos. Implicated in these formations is his fate or fear of fate. Never was there a creature more influenced by the slightest change in what he believes to be happening every minute. He wants to control fate, to divide and reassemble it, but he is its prisoner, even more than he is the prisoner of Mars.

"Where am I?" he asks ingenuously, wanting there to be some hope in the Countess' reply, though he knows their situation is exactly characterized by the fact of its being one without hope of any kind. She turns away.

The Astrologer allows himself to watch fascinated as the Countess rustles in her silk, straining as always to get away — from him, from Mars, from fate. She is sure that Astrologer, who reads everything, doesn't read her. To distract him and to allow them both to focus on their situation she begins to tell him again what he should already know.

"This garden is a part of the park of the Observatory of Parphar on a nameless island in the Hourglass Sea," she lectures. "It is the only intact space remaining on the island. We are marooned here, incorporated into the plan of the place like the statues we might as well be."

The Astrologer barely hears this discourse, gazing up determinedly into the eyes of the Countess as if through the ruined telescope that is the only other thing left on the island.

"No one is sure that they are real these days, least of all me," the Astrologer thinks to himself in a rare moment of clarity, "I know very well that I am my own worst enemy. The false logic of my statements and the imagined effects of houses and heavenly bodies have created a symbolic resonance that disorders meaning so violently as to shake the very foundations of pseudoscience. If a detached communication of ironic and secret metaphor is the primary coin of the realm we are in, the ineluctability of daily life makes it hard to actually do business here. At least for me."

He looks up hungrily. "Baby...," he begins aloud but again he falls into a state of strangely clear but silent inner knowledge.

"Fate," he goes on to himself, with a sense of discovery, "must be seen to have a secondary importance compared to its interpretation for the scheme to work at all. And the schemer, me, or someone, has to keep expectation alive for it to be consumed or destroyed in the money part of the equation. Normally I thrive on duplicity but now I find that I am what might be called 'in deep' with the Countess. I don't know how long I can keep it up or even stay awake. The monsters of heaven and those in my charts are nothing compared to the creatures contained in the Countess, but that is beside the point. Or at least it should not be part of the deal." He continues to look up at his companion, seeking a response in her dark eyes, though he has grown very silent in his thinking.

"There is a war in the sky or there was. We find ourselves between wars," he says to her. "And I find myself with you."

"Which is where I am lost," the Countess replies, looking away.

"The forms of the objects are all that is left to us," he says to distract both of them, though he himself is not sure to what he refers, so unused is he to the real world. He feels that he has slept perhaps a century in the lap of this foreigner, as he thinks of her.

"Do you really see them?" the Countess asks, not meaning the forms but thinking back to the theory of the many worlds. She knows that he has slept very briefly, if at all, perhaps experiencing only a suspension of consciousness or a cognitive dissonance generated by the unpredictability of her reaction to his display. In this moment, they share only their disorientation.

"Do you know what the forms are?" she wonders, more to herself than to him. She has given off believing him to know anything. "The forms may not be limitless, but then maybe they are," she continues. "You might be wrong. Astrologers are out of date beings," the Countess asserts against the rule of her apparent complicity in what might be thought of as this romance. "It is only because we are both prisoners," she murmurs. She has seen the trick, but believes herself to be in it for the forms, the equations, the beauty of them. As if in a trance, she begins to recite the many objects.

"Remnants, clusters, strings, fragments, trios, arcs, arches, hedrons — duos go without saying, have gone. Spiral, elliptical, irregular and just plain. These just plain formations are the ones one most relies on."

"The sky today. The unconscious stars." The Astrologer tries to bring her back to their conversation, his concept of the solar system, lucky stars, unlucky stars, guiding, morning and so on. "The physical sky, the mystic sky, the sky of lies." He is animated now. "We should open the book of the sky to the page of discord among the spheres, to a distant spot on the horizon. There are new Utopias or distant worlds," he says urgently to her, as if he hasn't always said it.

"Adventures in heaven," he says finally. She has heard this part before. Suddenly she hears a machine shudder somewhere as if running out of gas or air. She gasps and then breathes harshly out as if into a vacuum. A series of tiny explosions sounds in her ears, as if inside her head. She can't close her mind to them. She realizes that what the Astrologer means by repetition is something like blows to the head, but virtual. Again the sound sounds in her mind like a detonation. Again she breathes out.

"The Astrologer is on his own side," she says to herself, or perhaps he says it. His mouth is moving but his body is limp beside her as if he was asleep or dead. Something like a huge face appears on the horizon above them. It seems to be another moon or a satellite.

The Countess turns directly into this new moon. She knows that there is no future in this place and realizes about the past that it was also never there. She notices that she is still breathing out, as if every bit of her remaining breath were escaping from her body. She begins to feel seriously deflated and then, just as suddenly, she begins to breathe in, to take it all in, as if to consume the entire universe or at least this claustrophobic little island. She feels that she knows anew that she is an illusion, a construct, as is the Astrologer, useless now at her side. She wants to write — as if to right herself, to write herself off the island, though she knows this to be impossible. She has nothing to write with and so begins instead to compose and to recite, as if from memory, or as if reading her own mind like text:

"Bitter with sweet [quarrels]: in short that I who am always two myself, am myself (as you are) a war in which the planet is one with the sky [divided], in an illusive world. An illusion ahead of, behind, around and beside me, but I know you are that also, and that the writer is. I know there is a writer."

She stops and looks out at the sandy sea.

"That object on the horizon is a face. I think it is the face of the writer come to end it all," the Countess says, knowing that if true it would constitute a way out. The Astrologer is quiet, almost inaudible as he says, "I think I see it now."

Ada lays the story down beside Eddie who continues to sleep, or at least his eyes remain closed. She leaves, thinking herself effortlessly to the library, intensely energized by the story. When she arrives she finds that her paper screens are filled with the elaborate arabesques of *Ultravioleta*. Tired of the hopelessness of Mars, she gives herself gratefully over to viewing the progress of the great ship.

Ultravioleta

"And throws herself from the highest point. The parapet. Against her lover."

Pontius reads as Nahid writes. Nahid writes as she flies. He appreciates the delicacy of the story she is telling as she makes her way to *Ultravioleta*. He participates in her thoughts well before she knows she has entered the range of his own thinking. When Nahid finally sees the ship, she is stunned by the sheer size of it, awed by the neurodynamic perfection of the design.

"The mast divides the world," she notes, intuiting that the vast curve of the ship, stretching wildly back as it does, must give the passengers a sense of flight and a shape to their days. She sees them in her mind, disentangling themselves from something like rigging, falling as they think and read and write themselves into space.

"To The Gutenberg and beyond," Pontius startles her by answering her barely articulated question of where they are going. "Passengers include a human and a few clones. The humans are all Robinson actually. Hearty soul that Robinson. We lost a few." Pontius smiles. "And so we cloned him. Of course they are only virtual clones. There is sometimes a robot. Two I. We are going to the library and then beyond. We have gone about half a pot so far. Come aboard any time."

When they are not eating or dreaming, the bright faced Robinsons are framed by their little portholes. Human and I faces are indistinguishable, except when they are not. The robot wears his happy mask. As steersman, Pontius is taken up by his mechanical and psychic tasks. Like the ship itself he seems to be lit from within. Bits of text are visible in the makeshift walls of the decks and cabins just as the words that pour from Pontius' terrible mouth are at times visible on his almost human body.

"It takes a lot of coordinated thought to keep this baby afloat," Pontius reflects at the wheel. The emblematic function of the ship's wheel is typical of the equipment on board. In one sense a mere symbol, in another sense the wheel is crucial to keeping passengers and crew in the mood. One false move and they are likely to lose their train of thought and dissolve into real time. It can get ugly. Passenger travel on this scale is almost unheard of, but these Robinsons will do anything to travel. And then there is Marty.

It is understood that an I pilot will be close to his navigator, but with Pontius and Marty it goes beyond that. They find their relationship of oblivious but ironic enmity to be much more resonant, in terms of sheer mileage, than the usual attachment.

Marty thinks of his jobs as navigator, engineer and chief purser on *Ultravioleta* as half-time, though it is unclear, even to him, what this could mean. In Marty's work life, time seems to be halved and halved again and yet he manages to fill each of the shrinking halves with geometrically larger tasks. Like the painter who is his namesake, he finds a way of adjusting to his circumstances. He visualizes it.

"Whatever it takes," Marty says when he speaks at all.

Marty pursues the imaginary destiny of a painter marooned away from his time. He seeks the dislocation of occupying Xavier Martinez's life and his name and his nickname. Marty's life is a series of departures. He exploits its capacity to produce trouble in his artificially reconstructed heart. As any I, he lives best beyond himself in the invisible range of newly unknown outcomes to an already lived life. His activity isn't reliving so much as a relief from causality — a retreat into pre or anti-time.

"There are a lot of ways to go with a life, once you've got one," he thinks, looking back at the shrinking sun.

Unique among the I, Marty is more absence than presence, more observer than consumer. He watches the universe as it sweeps by. He watches out for the passengers, coddling, feeding, protecting them from the dangers of thought travel and the greater danger of being eaten by Pontius. Marty likes to eat but he prefers to paint.

"Color," he thinks, considering the pale stars.

As Marty looks out into the night he notices that one of the lights is moving. He realizes it is one of Pontius' current interests. Creating a mental space for her, he relishes her almost surprising arrival. When she appears it occurs to him that she is like Elsie in her self-containment, though her streaming black hair is in fact more like his own.

"Nahid," she says to his unasked question.

"Xavier Martinez," he responds formally.

"Jones," she adds, not looking directly at him.

"Marty," Marty says. "People call me Marty."

Escorted on board by this oddly comforting monster, Nahid curls into her paper cabin. She takes off her clothes and opens her notebook, settling in to write. The ship is hot with thinking but Nahid stretches out happily. She likes the heat.

Like the too bright sun of the future, *Ultravioleta* is a hot dense world. The air there is permeated with mental energy. The life force thrives as if it existed in an unlimited supply. The floodlight of alien hyperconsciousness fills the ship. It illuminates her passengers, invading their inner lives. The cabins have a paper door and a paper floor. The cells feel roomy but are shaped to the body. Curves of something like topographic lines repeat the curves of the ship.

The other human passengers, all Robinsons, are kept alive by Marty as purser. He relishes the role, providing as it does access to simple human hunger. Having installed Nahid, Marty tunes into a Robinson.

"Marty, could you think me up a burger and fries? I am sorry to interrupt your power revery with my tiresome human needs, but if you could see your way through to picturing some dill pickles this time that would be good. And if you could identify with a vanilla shake…"

Marty appears at the door with a tray at the same moment or slightly before the request event, hovering in the threshold like a waiter at the brink of chaos.

"Cheeseburger, Robinson?"

"Always a step ahead, that's what I like about you guys. I plan to have some pretty strong thoughts about these fries. You might want to stick around."

But it is already several days and many stanzas later. While mileage is a common concept and a unit of exchange, miles themselves are an anachronism here in this space where distance is officially measured in dreams, fits, stanzas and pots to piss in. The latter are the distance of the Earth to Jupiter run. That the I are not Jovian, as first thought, is generally acknowledged, but where they are from or how many pots they are able to think is unknown and possibly forbidden information, as no one can think of it for long.

Humans are known to consider the origin of the I and how far they can go to be the big downstream questions. Nahid lies on her bunk considering the problem. Humans, especially those who are Martians, believe that the answers will allow them to get their edge again, the edge they imagine themselves to have had and lost. Nahid is beginning to suspect that even the questions are wrong. She suspects that the I actually measure distance in the personal and idiosyncratic ways that they eat and sleep and live. She figures that they agree to these human interpretations of their measurements because they agree to everything. What they can't or won't do is to supply a straight answer to a simple question. It is evident that withholding information creates suspense, frustration and nostalgia — sometimes anger. She perceives that an I can get pretty fat in a setup as sweet as that. There are limits to how long such a situation can be maintained, but, she notes to herself, they can be fiddled with.

Nahid focuses again on her narrative.

"And throws herself from the parapet onto her lover who waits below, breaking her finger while he lies stunned…"

Pontius is on the bridge generating distance with Nahid's text. Fully focused, he dreams rapaciously into her mind, searching for the words she is about to write. He is surprised when he hears Marty in his own mind.

"Leave her alone you bitch." Fully frontal, Marty seems like a huge portrait of himself.

"Back off X."

Neither monster can tell if they are thinking or speaking aloud. Pontius and Marty circle each other mentally. The paper seems to blow out behind them and to readjust to the palpable waves of their engagement. Nahid and the Robinsons hover at their portholes like a silent chorus, open-mouthed. The ship sound is reduced to the small gasps they allow themselves. They know that dropping out of thought at this speed is worse than fatal. The effect works backwards obliterating the trajectory of life so completely it is as if one had never even wanted to travel. Never started out at all.

"We need her. It's not as if you've ever had a thought of your own. At this rate we'll never make it past the asteroid belt. There was that page down event." Marty is livid.

"Which knocked us…" Pontius leers at him.

"…that far back. Yes."

"So that explains what we are doing here and why the space inside is bigger than the space outside. It's that insatiable human hunger," Pontius pontificates.

Marty is surprised by the number of lies Pontius is able to tell simultaneously, but he knows he can't speak of it. "You should talk," he says instead. "How many have you had? How many lives? You are the hungry one. You are hunger itself."

"Of which me do you speak, Marty? What is your complaint? Look at the facts. The only truth is in action. You need to page down yourself, man. You need to keep up with current events."

"A true story," objects Marty, trying to move them forward, "produces ghosts." The ploy works. They can both feel the distance. The passengers feel it.

"The ghosts are the true thing," Pontius agrees. "The humans are the ghosts. The ghosts write the story. Nahid writes it. It's the step. It's the step she takes — the step the woman is willing to take for her lover, from the parapet." He considers the sacrifice as an action. It is his particular favorite. "And the sound of the word 'parapet,'" he goes on, reading now, "From the parapet and the tower. It's still there."

"It's here," Marty says, focusing the argument with a gesture. "The step is here." He brings his steepled hands to his chest, to where his heart would be if he had a heart. His familiar red scarf spills over them.

"I'm sick of dancing with you, pal." Pontius invokes their old hatred. Marty stands still relishing the hostility. There is nothing that is human in the consuming sigh with which he takes it in. It is always a pleasure for the I to feed on each other. Possibly his face disappears while his eyes and scarf remain for a second. The body he occupies interacts with the surrounding paper. There is a tearing, a perforation like a doll detaching from a pattern of dolls.

Nahid writes, holding her breath. She is aware of the danger of this struggle among the monsters to the Robinsons and herself, but knows of nothing else to do but continue to work. As she writes, Pontius continues to read.

"And so she steps out obliterating, for one man, the entire sky and sun, falling, floating, coming down. The tiny bone in her finger like a bird's wing breaks in one place. There is a drop of blood."

Where Pontius and Marty have contended, only negative space remains. *Ultravioleta* plunges into it.

Afternoon in Space

On leave from the ship and perhaps from his senses, Marty floats away. He works in the studio he maintains onhis own small ship, the *Elsie*. His trajectory runs parallel to *Ultravioleta*'s.

Marty knows more than he says. Marty paints himself to sleep. Space is what he thinks in — space in color. Color in trouble. The light of his remembered life shadows him as he relaxes into his imagined past. "Was it Elsie?" he thinks. "Was it really heaven or just the remembered gold of the hills?" Color of earth. Color of sun. Mentally he peers out into it. The yellow that once meant so much to him is white now. Just plain light. As I, he revels in himself, in his name, possessing all of his ages. Rage, irrationality, drunkenness, inspiration and anguish. They come out in color. Color into movement. Into light and time. Marty loves himself in time. He loves the bright chronic memories of his synesthesia.

He tells a story with light. Boy meets color. Boy loses color. It breaks his heart. It opens his eyes. He keeps track, noting everything, drawing it out. His heart fills with the action of colorless light. With writing. The calligraphy carries him along. The story changes according to the rendering. The story is about the moment of change. It is his recreation.

Afternoon in Marty's mind. The room is dark. A window fills with light. Elsie is the geographer of this brightness. She fills him with it in turn as if she herself emanates light. In this arrangement Elsie sits in space looking out. Her nebulous presence is the form the darkness takes as it proves itself inside of him. He makes claims against her. Against it. He claims she doesn't exist, can't assert. He thinks she can't prove her rules, but she knows it is the only thing she can do with them. He chases her out into the forest. He incarnates as rage. She holds him off with her tiny will.

Elsie was a fighter before she was a wife. Her father taught her to fight. She wins. She wins Marty. He pictures her illuminated by the afternoon. He drinks and sings. He paints. They peer together out across the hills to the bay, to the ocean and beyond. Marty sees the light as darker than it is. A fatalism underlies his charm. They have a daughter. They separate. Elsie and the daughter go away. They come back. Marty moves out. He teaches forever. He is an institution. He is alive with the perception of the darkness in the startling light around him.

Everyday light. He sees through it. He speaks with it. The light is especially dark where, when flooded with softness, there is a time of working and then dissolution. Marty is replaced by the universe. Reinhabited by the I, he remembers the dark. He wonders if he is more real as I or as he was. He wonders who is he to wonder that. A creature crawls across his mind. He puts himself out there. Something stops within and also around him as if about to pounce.

Out here afternoon is endless. An eternal delay frustrates night. Light fades from the inside out, leaving light inside Marty. His *approximate organs* generate more space than can be accounted for by Marty's mind. Space is invading him.

The cosmic hierarchy flatlines. Bells ring somewhere. Marty looks up as if to hear them with his eyes. Those can't be birds.

The Targets

Ada collects the facts. She gets the data from everyone's day, from the journeys and the wars, the time storms. Cap sends it. Everyone sends it, but only Cap is able to monitor her clonish participation in this thinking. It takes a robot to know what Ada knows. Cap and Ada watch as the anomalies and inconsistencies in the bodies of the thinkers parallel those in time. Variously the bodies die. Ada finds the deaths.

It is said of Ada that she began her work with the loss of flesh when the library itself became illegible to her. She lost her father to a war at the edge of an empire. Now she loses herself to its victims. She sees herself as a cause to their effect. They are the targets. She writes them. She counts them. There is absence in each citation, a zero in each death. She doesn't know why she does it. She knows only the facts and that she needs to organize and connect them. To present them.

Choosing a sequence with sound, Ada scrolls footage from early in the century. She freezes a moment. There is an explosion. Life spreads out over a landscape. There is a city. Parphar. People flying. When they fly, they become bodies. The bodies are not available. They have passed into history, but it is not generally possible to see them. Ada sees them because she has access. They are missing from the official record, insofar as there is a record left at all. Ada's access to what doesn't officially exist mimics her own status dating back to her illegal conception as a living logo. The theft of her identity seems to her not unlike the obliteration of theirs. She remembers the various thefts, the lives. Her life on the oxygen farm. Step parents. Step life.

There is an explosion of memory in Ada's head. Loud but not lasting. She feels dissociated from her memories. Hopelessly compromised by survival, she strives to ignore her life and focus on the information. She finds the facts. She finds them to be naturally concentric. They follow each other into circles. They become targets. The bodies are targets. For Ada, discovering this form is a form of rest, of redress. What she makes can be heard or seen. It can be read. She hears things. She remembers flesh by finding it in pictures. Painted, scrolled, heard flesh. She finds and arranges, absorbs and lists. She listens.

"Saturn drones as it rises," she hums. She searches for Cap in her mind, capturing additional information from him as he flies.

The time, she notes, is eighteen minutes past the hour, but what hour? She searches for the names. She lists them in columns. She bios them meticulously. Dreamily, she layers the information like skin, thickening their thin lives with facts. They seem to come from long ago and far away, though some died as recently as yesterday. Some of the victims are isolate, like the facts. Some are as connected as cousins to Ada and each other. Time is the only thing that is not relative now.

"What is a real target? What is not?" Ada goes on. "Is there an esthetic quality to this problem?"

She imagines that a horse is riding through her sleep, grazing around her headstones, invading her inner life. She wishes she had an inner life. She feels she has only a name. That she is a projection, that her memories are like scenes from movies. They say it is an effect from the war. The movies are like the war. Like the horse. Someone is the rider, someone the pilot, someone else the bombardier. She was the pilot. It was Mars. It was the war. One of the wars. It is very clear now.

"We were our own targets," she thinks. She remembers the explosions. People could fly. The acts of bloodless terror were finally seen as not enough. There was blood. It was expensive to make people die.

"We were searching for a place, a refuge for our love, but instead we were led to the land of the dead." She hears the line over and over.

She knows it is from the life of a writer. *Sayat Nova*. A movie or a memory. How can anyone know? The eyes of the woman are gray in a painting. Not unlike Ada's violet eyes. Her lace is painted. Filmed. The flesh in the painting is very natural. Looking up there is a lack of stars. It is this interminable dust. Set up a life. Watch it go down. Not to have been alive then. Not now.

"Saturn occults the sun." Ada continues to hum the words to a lost song.

The library explodes. Cap reels back but it is all in Ada's mind. Nothing can't be lost. Ada identifies the victims. She identifies with them. She accepts her life as a target. She believes that everywhere she is, the periphery fades.

"What are the facts?" she asks herself. "That I am designed to be in view," she thinks. "That I was made to win. That I have no talent, only power, that I have the talent to know it. That I steal everything from everyone. It is my job to give everything away. I have tried to give myself away, but there are no takers. Everyone wants to be taken by me and that's a fact," Ada reflects, not entirely without justification.

She finds herself considering the I, though generally she tries not to think of them. She thinks of Wyatt. With the exception of Wyatt, she thinks of the I as a waste of time. There is never anything new about them. She senses that they find her merely polite. They treat her like one of the boys. Wyatt says it is because, like them, she colonizes. Ada knows that when he says that he is putting it mildly. More than the I, Ada is an imperialist of her deal. She collects everyone and everything. She doesn't even try to seem real, at least not to them.

"Only to the few am I myself," she says aloud, resuming her work. "I am me to myself, to the dead and to Stella. We are attached. They want a patroness, a predeath agreement. A will. They know that my will is to save them from time. Stella knows. Their will is to bury themselves in my mind, but it's the same thing. Stella and I are the same," she decides for the thousandth time.

Ada, who finds everyone, is lost in her own mind. She looks out at the universe with her violet eyes, as if she were a stranger in it.

"She knows too much," Cap thinks as he flies on, engorged with facts, "It's not what you know but who you are. Not who you are, but where you go. Ada and Stella are not the same. Anyone could see it." He proceeds through space with his parallel conclusions. Cap longs to clear his palate with a kindred soul. One who knows nothing but knows it well. When he sees *Ultravioleta* on the horizon, he slows to the pure present.

"Martinez," he thinks.

The Face of Time

"I consider myself more of a painter than a robot," Cap transmits to Marty, without preamble, as he layers electronic color onto his face, remaking his visage with the deft yet heavy-handed skill required in the application of his trademark medium. Marty regards the results critically on the paper screen of the small craft which he has contrived for the occasional walk in the park, as he thinks of this kind of local thought travel.

"The red in the corner works for me," Marty says. "I like a darker look myself, but I think garish is good if you can carry it off."

They communicate intimately, screen to screen, face to face, page to page, though they are separated not only by many stanzas of space but by something resembling the Case Barrier. Marty is so far out of his own time as to be in a constant rebound mode. He would be a one-man time storm, if he were a man.

"Thanks. I thought of you with that red, my friend. For you, everything is dark — or I should say dark is everything. How goes it with the ship? Are you able to get any work done?" Cap asks with robotic politeness. "What do you call that little thing you are on? That's a pretty piece."

"Ah, this is the *Elsie* — what else could I call her? As for UV, at times it seems more like an anchor than a ship. Best place for *Ultravioleta* to go is down. Then I could finally work."

"The only thing is to paint and fly," Cap agrees.

"It's the only other thing," Marty responds. He thinks of thinking as the first thing or of eating, as a human might call the monstrous consumption by the I of others and of themselves that they think of as thinking. Marty regards Cap hungrily. Except for the intense emotional aura typical of robots, Cap is complacently indigestible to the I. Marty nibbles at the edge of him. Their artistic exchange has made him hungrier to work than merely to consume, strange as such a state is for one of the boys.

Marty seems to fade as he paints in his mind. He pictures the darkest of his paintings, the stars he almost included and then painted out, leaving only the pattern of the brush. He works over the painted stars again, point by point. He sees the movement of night against night, the suggestion of a long lost afternoon. Finally he includes light in the painting, negating even the darkness that was its dominant feature. The resulting picture suggests a blank screen but one with an infinite sense of depth.

"You will miss the boat," Cap observes.

"I do miss it, have missed it," Marty says. "The riggings are like the perspective lines in my work. Like the hands of a clock, they are there but you just don't think about them. Then they are gone. Everything is gone. Is that a sneer?"

"Sorry, no, I meant it more as a sympathetic but distant acknowledgement of intimacy. I do like the work, though I think you may have painted yourself into a corner with this one."

"No, man, I have painted myself out. Out is where I want to be — but I have to get back."

"And the government?" Cap brings up their other subject. "Where are they?"

"You mean other than yourself? On Mars I hear, trying to take over. And you, where are you?"

"I never know where I am," Cap says, picturing, however, his exact coordinates. "I know but I don't know that I know. The government knows things for me. I mean I am not the government any more than you are. It's just a job job for me. Like you and Pontius. You know what they say. Everybody has an asshole."

"Yeah, it's like the universe being inside out," Marty says, flying away.

"Come again?" Cap says.

"In my piece — I plan to call it *The Face of Time*. In it, the darkness is the thing that shines."

But Marty's focus is elsewhere now. Cap sees him fly away, his scarf streaming to one side of his perfect little craft in a decorative red wave. Cap follows Marty with his mechanical attention. *Ultravioleta* looms to fill his screen. When he begins to feel the scrutiny of Pontius, Cap backs off, fitting himself neatly into the thoughtful wake of the great ship.

The Spicer Decision

Wyatt flies the *Stella*. He arrives alongside *Ultravioleta* in space if not time. He is almost unseen and unheard except when he steps back into his past. Even then it is only Ada who registers a small ripple in the continuum of time. Only Nahid who looks up for a moment from her work.

Doc Holliday returns for his due. He has the quality of what never was. The patterns of life, permanently stamped on his face, are not present in his heart which is strangely empty. Like a fountain instead of a pump his heart seems to flow out, draining him. He lays his cards on the table. Doc's heart is a fountain of love. His love for the next card supercedes his love even for Wyatt who he sees as entirely equivalent to his own being. His regard for Wyatt is the closest he has ever come to taking care of himself.

"Go for broke," he remembers saying to Wyatt before the fight and before they went in on the bar and later when they took over the town. It was never about events and plans. Holliday doesn't live in the world but in the game. He lives for Wyatt. For the doctor, Wyatt is more than life. He is a way to pass the time. He is continuity and destiny. He is luck.

Wyatt thrives on the strange hot sun of this Tombstone love. His opinion of the doctor is as golden as the teeth Holliday once pounded into the mouths of his fashionable clientele. Partner, mirror, brother, Wyatt watches the doctor die. He regards Holliday's nearness to death as nearness to himself, to his own death and the death of the world.

The game and its variations all militate against their having any awareness of time. Time exists only in the inevitable death of the sacred dentist, his Romantic sinking into toothless nonentity. Wyatt knows that Doc's decisions are like those of the poet Jack Spicer, much later in time. They are always to wait on the game — to wait for the next drink, the next card and the next line, quietly saying yes to death, as if it would solve all of his social and business problems.

Holliday sings the words of his favorite song to himself and coughs a little blood. He is a tragedian frozen on a stage. Wyatt elopes with the idea of him, every time they meet. The doctor, who rarely moves unless to draw his gun or play his cards, runs wildly off with Wyatt's heart. They go far out on the range together with their manly talk. The doctor brings it back by visibly dying a little more each moment, by inches and eons, his vest gold, his hair golden, all about him shining, perspiring, expiring.

"Tom, that property next to the cemetery, just outside of town, I want you to get that for us and I want you to use this to do it." He begins to stack fifty dollar gold pieces on the table. A hush settles over the already quiet bar. "I want you to use these winnings. Invest 'em, so to speak, in that little spot. Nothing's there now but in the future you never know how it might come in handy. A bit of territory between Boot Hill and the gallows might be pretty sweet down the line. Nice to put something up there where so many are brought down."

"Where the souls wander," Wyatt concurs. "That corridor where the souls of killers and horse thieves and the like are released pending their entry into hell. Or heaven — unlikely as that may be. Might be a good place for a strip mall." Doc looks at him quizzically. "An all night general store, you know, in case folks need some little thing unexpectedly."

"I never have any idea what you are talking about but I do love to hear you talk." Doc settles into his little cigar, coughing and chuckling inwardly, throwing back a shot. "Never have the slightest notion what you are gettin' at. No siree."

Wyatt sits back also, the gold in a lovely pile between them, he contemplates their prospective property. All the fighting and strategizing they have done to get themselves where they are for an empty spot outside a half-dead town. "Life on earth," he thinks. "There's nothing like it."

Deliverance

Ultravioleta is delivered like a letter. Ada watches as the big ship arrives in perfect time. Waltzing out of melodic space into the silence of the library, descending the stairs from the stars, her sails spread out in an arc twice the size of any vessel ever seen in these parts. Like a paper cradle rocking passengers and crew inside her, *Ultravioleta* breaks into a spectacular fall. Ada provides the mental net, easily folding the vast craft into the atrium of the enclosed but limitless space of the library.

"As the soul's place of origin and eternal destination, cosmic space is imbued with a maternal sense," Ada murmurs to herself. "Here they come, drenched with space," she adds, watching as the passengers spill from the ship. Some fall on their faces, some on their asses. As expected, many have the delusion they are visiting their mothers. Others that they are mothers themselves, regardless of gender. Artists and mothers creating space — so they imagine themselves as they enter the Europan sphere of influence. So Ada acknowledges them as she talks them down, one by one.

"The Eternal Maternal" is the subject of her acclimating narrowcast. Group travel has resulted in the usual blending. The passengers look for Ada, as, continuing to believe they are descending, they try to sort themselves out. The various Robinsons fold into a single Robinson whose head aches with a sense of his multiple pasts.

"Remember us?" he says.

"I meet a lot of people," she replies, gathering the stragglers. Ada is unwilling, for now, to acknowledge her acquaintance with Robinson. To her, all of their little faces look the same as each other and as every other traveler's face, even the ones she is supposed to know.

"Spaced," they say sleepily alighting onto the glossy wooden porches of the paper atrium of The Gutenberg. Ascending its grand staircase, they squint up at the decorative gold capitals shining down from what is said to be a dome of pure crystal. They think about the dome and wonder who they are and where they are. And then they think they know. Ada knows it is all just atoms, like much in space, but maintains the composure of a professional host, agreeing to everything, accepting their compliments, doling out her own.

"Welcome," she murmurs into each ear and goes on to whisper wordlessly to them in I, giving her guests the sense of dislocative panic so valued by the seasoned traveler.

Pontius floats past, saluting Ada's "Finely flown." And Marty nods to her "*A bientôt*," acknowledging their acquaintance in Paris a lifetime ago.

Ada finds that one of the humans, Nahid, having landed upright, is already trying to access the card catalog. "There is so much I need to know right away," Nahid says, barely looking up from the scroll open in her lap. Her black electric hair falls around her like a veil.

Robinson announces that he has a date.

"That explains the presence I have felt," Ada replies. "I didn't realize you were with the current consort of *herself*, though of course I should have known."

"Well, I consort when I can," he says, growing fuzzy as he prepares to enter the space he shares with his mate, as he thinks of her. Ada and Nahid, sitting together, watch as he ascends.

"I see what she gets from him but I don't know what he sees in her," Nahid says as she and Ada exchange looks.

"Don't ask," Ada wills their attention back to each other and to the books that are opening like flowers in their minds.

Nahid turns to this research unable to believe her good fortune in being able to enter into the thick of it with Ada right here in this magnificent lobby. Ada finds herself to be charmed by this little Earthling. She senses Nahid's fated trajectory, as much as she does those of the other guests, but for now she allows, as always, full access to the collection.

Nahid gets out an elaborate pen and applies herself to her scroll. Ada mentally follows the notes as she takes them.

"The mysterious return of Captain Nemo found in the archives of the *Echo of Cities*. Like Jupiter's bird. Impact craters Pwyll and Callanish. *This Was Tomorrow*. Propelled by language there. Here," Nahid corrects.

Ada realizes that Nahid is reconstituting her attention by sectioning off bits of the present. She admires the technique while allowing for its limits and dangers, not the least of which is the problem of knowing too much too soon, closely followed by the one of a little knowledge and then there is the one of getting in over your pretty little head.

"Radio is an alteration of space and a structuring of time. *Toward a Political Phenomenology of Listening.* Tangled I was…but was given to rely on Luther…my direct heart…a fictional *novum* validated by cognitive knowledge. Clouded by the present wave of irrationalism…*New Maps of Hell.* The new framework is correlative to the new inhabitants."

"Ah, the controlled irrational," Ada comments. "Nice."

"The Galilean Moons of Jupiter — Io, Europa, Ganymede and Callisto — were originally called the Medicean planets. Simon Marius discovered the moons earlier but did not publish his findings. All are inhabited but we don't know by whom. Only the I know or so it is said," Nahid writes. "We don't know how many were saved," she continues, accessing an historical node.

"Correct," Ada responds.

"This is not simply an error; this is a devilish error in strategy." As Nahid continues to make notes, the real focus of her research becomes apparent to Ada, who knows it won't get her where she wants to go. "But she has to move through it," Ada thinks.

"Careful," she chides as Nahid glances up at her, sidelong. "You will go too far, too fast, little one." But she allows the library to hold nothing back. Nahid goes on, writing very quickly now.

"After the Clone Wars, especially III and IV, on Mars, the difference between fact and fiction, or among the various fictions, grew less important. Less clear. Martians became more adept at manipulating the physical qualities of information even as or perhaps because their methods were limited by the resources. The Maryolatry's Information Imperatives actually failed to eliminate any abuses, but offered a program and an inspiration to those who would alter history in advance of its being written. The Mary methods changed the old ways of determining the social order. The questions of who was a collaborator and of what constituted espionage or sabotage all became more difficult to answer. There was a sense of replacement, a letting go of the past, of the idea of the past, with the anguish of a child letting go of her mother's hand."

Nahid gazes up at Ada, flattered by her attention. In synchrony, they think into stacks rarely touched by visiting beings, still less by tiny human scholars. They understand together what would not have been clear to either alone. They wonder to themselves what they are hearing when they think in unison. They tell themselves a story of what was happening then. What now.

"A counterfeit faith that on the surface looks like the genuine article," Nahid lets her pen write thoughtfully. "No one can travel that way," she objects aloud.

"No, not far," Ada agrees. "Not beyond the first Case Barrier just past Mars. Inner becomes outer life in a situation like that. There is a danger of dropping out of thought into real time. There are a thousand ways to die. The skilled traveler coasts just below consciousness, skating along it, emerging, falling back. Not awake but not not. Not asleep because sleep can kill at that velocity. There needs to be a sense of harmony with ambient sound. Bursts of dissonance. A regularity. The whine of the alloy. Gold with gold. The doubloon. Bite down hard, as you know."

Nahid is speechless as she struggles to write everything down, overwhelmed by the library, by the librarian. She is unable to calculate how far she might travel on this rich new information.

Ada feels drawn into this research but, aware of her duties as concierge, she leaves Nahid reluctantly and returns to her other guests. The air is charged. Clouds of interstellar dust fills the inner space of the library like new love. Ultraviolet energy causes it to glow like a bulb.

Married

"I alone. Nameless I," is the thought, though the thinker is not alone, but married, and everyone knows her as Mary. She is I, one of the boys but female, not Mary to herself or to Robinson to whom she is M. M is pure I.

"Form with itself content," Robinson muses, penetrating the perception barrier surrounding his mate. It is his will, his fate, to be fully fascinated, fully fastened to M — like a moon to a planet or like any of the heavenly bodies to each other. He knows it is the only way to survive a relationship with Herself as she is also often called.

Circling The Gutenberg as the satellite circles Europa which itself circles Jupiter, Robinson orients himself in what he perceives to be one of the endless orbits that is typical of their meeting places. He is not bothered by the impossibility of being where he is. In some lives, the impossible is given. In some lives, being present, possible or not, is enough.

"Form without form and yet fully formed," Robinson comments appreciatively. Robinson is acutely aware that M's changeable beauty affects him like an addictive poison. He often concludes that not being killed by it, by her, is a full time job, the only one for which he is really suited.

Robinson has his usual thoughts. He watches as M reveals herself. As she becomes embodied and imposing, she imposes, turning dangerously toward him. Robinson's ability to innovate in extreme environments allows him to make the first move in what passes for their conversation. Or so he believes. In fact his every move is a response to a predatory gesture of his lover. Each I is a hunter. Each interlocutor always already cooked in their minds. Conversations create affective fields the effect of which are nuanced according to the quality and intensity of the creature in question.

His ability to survive would make Robinson delectable to any I. M is no different. To the degree to which any I can love, she loves his exquisite attention. She finds his flaws and irregularities delicious. His ability to survive the scrutiny with which she isolates her prey is sustaining and dependable, but only just.

As an I, M's experience of herself is complete. Wyatt once commented to her "I see myself alone." "But of course," she had thought, "and so do I."

Though married, M and Robinson see themselves as single, singular though entwined. Theirs is a perfect relationship. They both know it, but they know it separately.

Her abbreviation is his idea. He relates to M as the letter he has selected to be her designation. It is an honorific, a diminutive, an expression of the familiar "you" unavailable to him in the language of the I in which every "you" is a formal victim. M is thou to him most dear. I is thou in his universe.

M is essentially formless, though she seems to take form at times. Her formlessness allows Robinson to be unsure of who or what he loves. He feels he is in love with her or at least with the letter of her. He says to himself that it is her indeterminate femality that fixes him. The peculiarly unfixed state recognizable as their passion seems to have little to do with gender, but then it does. He experiences his love as an adjustment, an accommodation, moment to moment.

"M," he says, drawing her out, humming her to himself. "Where are you, darling? How are you? What are you?" He finds her. "What are you doing? Where is Cap? Have you been with that damn robot again?"

"He is a machine," M's expression is slightly interested but unsympathetic, silent, changeable. It has its usual impact on Robinson.

"I hardly ever see him," she lies complacently. "And I am hungry," she says though she doesn't exactly talk.

"Not full like me," he thinks, "with you."

"No, not," she returns. "Not full. Not with you. Not full but hungry. I want something to eat, something to be. A new line. A new look," she goes on, casting about her. "A way away. I want a way out."

"We will just get a line on the Marys, then," he says, "We will have to get you in touch with the ladies. That's what we'll do. Those babies really get around. The solar system is like a sewing circle to them. It is just a matter of time before they leave it behind — my opinion. Of course if you are looking for a way to go farther, faster — but what could that mean for you? How gone do you want to be?"

With enormous effort and restraint M manifests in robes of thought that flow uninterrupted from her shoulders, down her back. She twists toward Robinson as a winged thing. Female, feathered, enclosed and vast. Demanding. His passion waits holding and filling. Feeling. Falling. She lands on his heart, all claws. He holds her back. She wants to go on. He seems to come up for air out of her face. He sees himself through her eyes.

"What can it mean when you never speak?" he complains, but he knows what it means. There is a heat to her apparent skin. A coolness to her eyes, to her gaze which he is caught in. He is caught inside.

"What can it signify, Mary?" he repeats, as she, widening her span, already wide, speaks with her eyes, releasing him. She sighs and rustles in place. In space.

"Okay, I read you."

He feels now just how far she wants to go. He sees that her passion will be identical with the distance gone, with the fact of traveling itself, with the thought of movement through thought, of movement at all.

"I want," she says again. "I want to hear and see and taste myself moving away. I want out and gone."

"Sure baby." Robinson sees himself as the grease in this lightning. The only way to make her stay is to help her go. It is basic to their relationship. It is what holds him — that and her unearthly beauty.

"Anything you say," he says.

He removes himself from M's mental grasp and gives some thought to this little excursion. Mentally he gets in touch with Ada and starts to think through the problem with her, exploiting the history they have. This time Ada responds easily to Robinson. Many have a history with Ada, but it can be said of she and Robinson, at least, that they went there and back. Dreamily they allow themselves to remember the coming, the going back. They produce the distance with the memory.

"Ada is not so Mary as to be impossible but is definitely in touch with the ladies," he thinks to himself, though he knows his mind to be fully invaded by at least two consciousnesses. He notices that his wife is glowering deliciously, closing in on him now that his attention is slightly turned from her. He turns it back.

"I'm not really malleable, you know," M mutters under her breath, growing dark.

Ada is already on it. She believes this virtual fly-by is the perfect way to hasten Stella's arrival at the library. Responding to her request, Stella and Tinia have suited up in their minds and, firing on all synapses, lead a fleet of imagined Marys into M's vicinity. They appear also in Robinson's mind. He figures that after she goes off with them, M will return, but he never knows. That's the drill. Or maybe it's only the perception barrier and she never really goes anywhwere. He can't tell. He looks away, feeling satisfied but bereft. Feeling crushed by the paper wings of the Marys, already swooping down.

M rises, formless hand held to her formless heart, eyes closed, already gone.

Stella's Approach

Emotional obsession, effective for getting one in deep, is notoriously unstable as a method of moving through space and time, but Stella rarely travels any other way. Closing in on the library but still out far, she is beginning to break up or down. Like anyone encountering Europan space with its intersecting orbits, its thick imaginary dust, its conflicting times, Stella experiences a local version of the old problem of the many worlds.

"But everything is local," Stella thinks as she sinks. She thinks of Wyatt and uses the thought to gain some extra velocity, jeopardizing her mission and sanity by opening herself to her old lover and stalker.

"Or whatever he is," Ada watches with perfectly delineated attention that is exact, even for a clone. Without object, without doubt, she waits for Stella.

"He buys me with your love," Stella explains, willing herself even further out. "The contract is sweet. I find you. I find Ada. My absent one. My imaginary one. It's better than nothing. If another war comes we will take it up again. Like last time. Ready to go. Ready to eat. Me, Nemo. No one. Nothing. Ready to eat. Ready to die, but then that's me. I am a soldier. My interpretations are based on desire. I was wondering when you'd see it."

Stella falls through space like a stone. At this rate, Ada is unsure she can talk her down in one piece. "You are much too fast," she mutters, adjusting herself to the implacable emergency of Stella's approach. "How much farther will you go?" More to herself than to Stella.

"How much farther can I get? Once you know something you know or are known by it until you forget everything or are otherwise destroyed. But who will know about us? I don't manipulate you in order to survive but because I can," Stella insists. "The results are unpredictable but there are results. It is a way of being close. You are simply the subject matter. You wouldn't believe it if I told you who first said that to me."

Dangerously, Stella falls asleep. She wakes up listening. She searches for Ada, scanning the universe with her mind. She antagonizes the Wyatt in her head.

"Who does he think he is?" she says. "Where does he think he is going?"

She flies crazily.

"Where am I? Why Wyatt? Why not? What kind of man is he? What constitutes a song? When he invades me does he invade us? What kind of fool am I? Are we wrong to believe in him? Am I? We represent or at least I represent. That's what. That's why. We represent our governments as emissaries or examples. That is what we said. But do they really have a government? Do we? With whom have we agreed? How can you make an agreement with a constructed identity? And yet, how can you not?"

Stella leans into a steep dive. Ada watches. Calculating her chance, she spreads open the walls of the library like a lotus. The paper curls and shreds like dust. Like pollen. Like stars. "Stella like stardust. No, not quite right," she remembers. "Like light. She is mine. Also not quite." The wooden shelves of the library gleam in Ada's mind. The books open. The lines break. The words seem to dance off the pages.

"And the other things. The physical things," Stella rants. "How can we eat? Where did we get this food? Was it ever offered to an idol? Is this only about eating? About hunger? Who or what is the food in this situation? Are they gods? Are they demons?"

"Shut up," Ada says but feels like she is speaking to herself.

"I am always outward. Having torn out." Stella continues. "Having had something torn out of me. The I make history seem inevitable. They tell it like jokes. They get it. They have a lot to say. They are a thought machine. They are me and god knows they are you. No I take that back. They are not me. There is a hole in me where history should be. Wyatt fills it. He wants to. I am irresistible to him. To them. Me with no history. No resistance. No history but the war. No war but with you. My love. Our love. Our war."

"Stella! Stop — no. Don't stop but don't go. Don't go on! But wait, yes, go on! Go on!" Ada hears herself cry, knowing at this rate of contradiction she will kill them both. Stella seems to take up the whole sky, flying very low, screaming at the top of her voice.

"The inside of my head expands until it feels like there is no room for my soul. There is a fuel dump and a mind meld. Metabolism is elongated. Embolism a syllable away. Ready to eat. Only just not this time, thank you Jesus. Across another barrier. Wyatt doesn't know what he has done. Then he does. He does it some more. He goes. Into a universe of separate stones. Sleeps again. Wakes in anguish."

"Please," Ada tries. Stella takes it down a notch.

"He works by reversal. I work by reversal. My body in space. In the air, when there is air. In paper. On it. I have it on paper. The air caught in this paper lung breathes me. Never enough air. Paper tears. The metal air. The gold is cold. Peep hole into nothing. My particular skill. My skull."

"Listen to me. This is normal," Ada lies carefully, adding facts as needed for distraction. Here, she knows, it is be distracted or die. "You are here. You have arrived. You have negated space. The negation has created an oscillating series of spiral symmetries. They have interlaced in discrete units of quasi-reception like rhetorical statements. Actual questions. Under the pattern is a pattern. You fall forward. You fall back. Again. An implosion. A chorus of sirens. That roar in your head is your obsession with your work. With work in general. The only way to kick the I thing. Work through it. You did it. You did good. You are back."

Finally like a bee to a flower, Stella is down. Ada sees her safely into The Gutenberg, into her room, her bed. Stella drops happily into the paper cot in her new space. Transparent as ever, she seems to sweat gold. Nothing like a freshly laid out hotel room. She looks out and dreams, holding it all in her head.

"Mars of iron," Stella muses, though she is looking out at Jupiter. She dreams of a Martian hotel. "That old fire escape was attached to the window like a strand of DNA. Europan elegance from the last century but one. Old Europe. A dream in space. A scheme of understanding. I understand them. I understand you. I understood him. Wyatt. He is you in that sense. Cessation of interior monologue. Human mirror. Deflection of fire. No fire. No escape. New radio in the new place. Weather when you need it. A moon obliterates Saturn."

"Ganymede or Calisto," Stella reasons, stretching herself out, dazedly, staring at one of the moons. The window looms. Stella wakes. Ada hovers over her in thought, warm like a sun and like the real sun, at this distance, cold. Ada says, "I am not saved from you, from him, from being stalked. You are not alone in being stalked by him. He is Nemesis to me as well as to you. Lover to my lover. He is the predator that springs. He stops my heart, tears my throat. Something sacred to me, let's call it my death, is not available to him. That oneself is taken. Not like life with its proximity, its need for itself. Death changes when clones and women die, when I die. When you know that I am not like you, I simply die."

Ada stays with Stella, waiting to hear her say something more, something else.

"Fly away, as an eagle, toward heaven," Stella says, knowing she must.

"But that is what you always say," Ada replies.

The Legend of Dinner

The thinking is loud at the table. Ada considers her guests, willing them to her side and into their places. Pontius winds himself into a chair looking, as always, too large for his situation. He seems to redden the air around him like dye pouring into a river. He and Ada lock eyes and he settles into colorless silence.

"Beast, Pontius?" she asks, passing him the vegetable meat on its bone china platter. Reaped from the cryopits of Mars, this cross-genre delicacy is done to a turn, violet to a deep purple, not unlike Ada's eyes. Nahid, in her corner, follows the reflection of the china on the glossy wooden table, almost not daring to look into the dangerous gazes of the monsters who are her fellow guests.

"The beast is better than perfect," Pontius comments. "It is slightly off, giving it a certain piquancy. Beast can be so boring if it is merely excellent. Don't you agree?"

"Of course you would expect it to be good and it is given that the expected is predictable and I know it might not be exciting to eat something that has not been, in some sense, had by you and that further has nothing to say," Ada says, as Pontius passes Wyatt the beast along with its translucent boat of pink gravy. "And yet a thing that was born to be eaten can be soothing to the digestion, I also find."

"Ah, but it speaks to me," Wyatt says, taking the plate. "It tells a tale of vegetative gladness, of birth and death being the same, of beings who are food and of eating as being. If this beast was any better I would think I had died and gone to heaven. Isn't that what they say?"

"I say that or I have said it," says Nahid who passes on the beast, finding it too purple, vegetable or not. She passes it to Tinia who feels too happy to eat, but who likes to drink. Tinia takes a drink. The glasses on the table shimmer hypnotically. Robinson gets the platter next, holding down the far end of the table with Dayv. Dayv takes a huge piece, as does Robinson. Tinia beams. Robinson fidgets.

Stella and Wyatt are not near each other at the table but the intensity of their lack of eye contact creates a palpable energy. Pontius edges into it. Ada frowns, directing herself to Wyatt.

Wyatt and Ada don't need to talk to speak. No one does. But here, where a rearrangement of atoms counts as a comment, each exchange of glances between them electrifies the party. The table, in turn, seems to separate itself from time. As always in space, thought exists visibly, if one has the will to make it appear.

Ada lets herself think about the war and then everyone thinks about the war. There is a sense of panic or dismemberment or dis-remembering. Ada turns to Robinson on her left who turns to Nahid on his. They seem to flinch simultaneously and sigh, their visible breaths mixing with splattered images. Dust and glass, people and animals drift across the table like a mirage. Tinia's eyes widen like a screen. Marty enters late, settling himself, he brings his folded hands to his chest, where they rest in front of his red scarf. He is very quiet. Wyatt and Pontius stretch themselves out, getting measurably larger.

"Space seems," Robinson says, "unusually viscous or it did as we approached Saturn and since we have arrived, especially since we have arrived here at the table. Like a pinkish soup actually or something like…"

"Like blood." Wyatt comments, helping himself to more gravy. "Like blood. Blood," he goes on, "is what we like. It is what they are like." He alludes to what everyone knows about the legends of vampires on Mars. Dayv smiles. He watches Wyatt and Stella with avid interest. The connections occurring at the table along with the cultivation of this kind of legend are making for a social occasion of almost incalculable value in terms of sheer accumulated distance or nutritional content, not to say sweetness. Tinia, hyper-aware, as always, takes it in, with the rest of her tea, unsure which is more intoxicating. Her glass rings against the china as she sets it down empty.

"There is another invasion," Tinia repeats what everyone knows. "Or maybe it's a civil war. The living against the dead or the undead against each other."

"Mars," Pontius rolls the word around in his mouth. "The war on Mars, it is where we live when we are home."

Nahid sighs against what seems to her this strange speaking about the Martian wars.

"Many try to suck the life out of Mars," she says. "You don't have to be supernatural to do it."

Ada and Stella regard Nahid from their ends of the table. As usual, Stella is both naked and transparent. Both gold and silver. She glows appreciatively with what she perceives to be the arch negativity of this neophyte.

"You are a Mary then?" Wyatt asks Nahid, knowing she is not.

"I would aspire to have the heart of a Mary," Nahid replies, feeling the heat of his attention, "if it were not presumptuous to say so in the present company."

"Nicely put," Ada comments in a thought audible to half the table. Pontius and Wyatt have Nahid in their crosshairs. She takes it well but there is a noticeable marshalling among the Marys.

"You boys on your way back to Mars?" Tinia seems to uncoil herself. "Personally I was hoping to go on out to the end of the system, while we have the talent on board. I mean if we do."

"Anywhere you want to go, darling," Robinson offers, in spite of his mere humanity. "Just say the word."

"The war on Mars makes itself felt everywhere, especially now. Bring it out to the end of time. Travel on it. Why not?" Ada speaks for the table. "Bring it home. Will the war change your home if you have one? Or will Mars change in our lifetimes, those of us who have lifetimes?"

"That time is incommensurate for us is understood," Stella adds, eyeing Wyatt. "They say there is no real time among the I, and yet I have heard there is."

"Of course there is," Wyatt begins. Pontius bristles. Ada observes that he directs himself to Stella whenever he speaks and that there is a bloody tinge to Stella's aura.

"If you bring the war home," Stella goes on, posing the familiar questions, "where are you? Where is home? Is there a history there? Have you something to do with your own history? Or with ours?"

"I know that we seem…" Wyatt tries again.

"You do seem," Stella interrupts. "You do strongly seem to affect seeming. Or to control what is perceived. Do you change or determine what happens?"

"It is unthinkable to any of us at the table who thinks of themselves as a person — it is unthinkable to the people," Robinson interjects, "that what is thought of as history is a story manipulated to achieve a desired effect. How can that still be true so long after the many times we have known it? What of the Information Imperatives? Didn't they mean anything? Can we escape from our destiny by simply removing ourselves from our place of origin? From our time?"

"But we enhance time," Pontius claims loudly. "We replace time with something better. Sure it's a little dangerous but there is nothing in the Imperatives to prevent this type of enhancement. It is clearly…"

"Case in point," Ada interrupts, halting the mental waves about to overwhelm the table. Knowing that only she can stop this conversational takeover, Ada goes into a directed revery.

"Like any clone, I am a fatalist." Ada's thoughts are silent but audible to everyone. Effortlessly, she fixes their attentions to herself. "I know there is no escape, though I have myself apparently escaped many times. I remember what it is to arrive somewhere. The starting over. The effect of one's same old mystique on the new ones. Hoping that an unknown interlocutor will provide a rewarding exchange, as if anyone could." She looks at Stella. "As if anyone ever does."

Ada is allowing the barrier between inner and outer life to break down. The I at the table observe this move appreciatively, seeing the merging of things recapitulated in the depths of Ada's violet eyes.

"You are I," they think in concert with Ada and each other.

"No, not I, not you," she responds, smiling her professional smile. "I am like Nahid here, only not so happy or so young. Like her I have the need to make the world out of the work. This used to be called art. Now it is called travel or simply thought. The media I use are various and, as with war, the effect depends on the speciation of your, ah, readers or — what shall we call them? — your participants? You never know what you will get or what you will get back when you put something together. In the present instance the dinner is the work."

She looks out at her guests whose attentions she consumes as they consume their beast and their tea. She looks at Stella again.

"It's like being a traveler or a soldier," she continues. "Or a lover. It's about the barriers. The Case Barrier is no more real than those between you and I," she looks up at Wyatt, "meaning that it is either a mortal danger or entirely a figment of our imagination."

Wyatt follows her thinking hungrily. For a moment, Ada sees herself reflected in his black eyes. Stella's preoccupation with Pontius has made Ada and Wyatt into a couple, albeit an unhappy one.

"Mars always changes. Like as gold in the fire tried... Mighty Mars the red." Wyatt rarely quotes himself but now he does. "You are right to think of them — the war and the barriers. The Case Barrier is a myth just like the war. The war overwhelms the cosmos like it does Mars. It is a universal war that is always going on."

Everyone looks up at this.

"Tell us more of this universe?" Stella speaks for the table. "Of this war."

They all feel they have left time, though they had not believed themselves to be caught in it at this moment. A horizon not previously seen falls away. To Stella it is as if the once impenetrable Case Barrier was being crossed by their thinking. No one breathes. No one eats. There is a strange sense of joy waiting for Wyatt to speak. The table believes he is about to say something new — now that the Barrier has been removed. Pontius narrows his enormous eyes against the inevitability of this conversation. He has suspected where Ada was going with her thinking and was ambivalent about it, though no one could deny it was a tasty moment.

"Wars do obtain," Wyatt begins, "because everywhere there is an unevenness of the ability to imagine war or peace and the power to imagine wants to flow evenly through space like light but is drawn in by the force of the imagination as if by — as if by gravity, I suppose. This kind of imagination is bent and tends to destroy what could be thought of as life. The universe is full of life, full of beings who can die. They think of war and they die."

"So people are as numerous as stars?" Nahid says, as if to herself. "And there are no barriers?"

"Yes. No. Not exactly people, but yes. The Case Barrier itself is alive, to the degree that it exists at all. I mean to say it speaks. They speak, for it is multiple like us. It is us, really. It is I, like everything."

Ada continues to interrogate Wyatt with her eyes. She doesn't speak. She can't express her suspicion of this crowded universe in endless war. As always with the I, this startling revelation is finally just speech, their conclusion that everything, that anything, is I is all too familiar.

"Is there thought?" Stella asks, meaning travel.

"The universe can be perceived as entirely made of thought," Pontius says, seeming to animate again, having become quiet in the face of Wyatt's assertions. He draws near to Stella. "Or it is possible that as thinkers we can only find it legible that way."

"Are they small?" Nahid asks.

"There are small ones." Wyatt engages with her as a seductive father. His raw display of power is somehow more noticeable than the information that there are small previously unknown beings somewhere.

"How small are they?" Robinson asks. "And who are they? and where? Would you tell us if you knew. Is this a trick?"

Pontius and Wyatt turn to him surprised, "When have we ever lied to you?"

The humans at the table all sigh. Even Dayv sighs.

"Is there a thinking among you, then, about us?" Ada pursues Wyatt, notwithstanding Pontius' electrifying focus on Stella. The I rarely refer to themselves as we. Ada recognizes this defensiveness as an unusual opening. "Is there a thinking about those of us in what was until now the known universe?" she adds.

But they all know it doesn't matter. Whenever there is a government or other authority there is usually a demand for quantity, for technology. But the I, traveling as they do through thought and attention, living through people, through each other — eccentric, addicted to love — the I have the great authority of the first person but without law or numbers, without metal. They stop nothing, start nothing but seem to have been present in the interstices of every event since it was first perceived they were present. They *are* presence. They are not in charge, but everything seems charged by them. Everyone feeds them, as Ada does now.

The dessert course arrives. It is sweetened air. Soon the table floats on a no cal sugar high. Away from the table, staring into space, Dayv muses to himself how good it is that simple sugar can create actual happiness. He looks out at Jupiter but sees Mars besieged in his mind. "There is only sorrow there," he thinks. "Why are people attached to that red place of anguish? Why are there always Martians?"

"It is good to be here with you," Tinia whispers in I, standing very near to Dayv. "I am so glad you are here," she repeats. They look out at Jupiter, considering the implications.

The party begins to dissolve. Those who are not I feel they have farther to go now that the universe has opened like a door. The humans present want to escape from Mars, from the Mars in their minds. Ada reads them as they rise from the table. She hands them off each to the other in her mind.

"The beast was good," Stella whispers as they embrace for a moment. "But the beasts are better," she laughs, going.

Ada is very still as she watches Pontius follow Stella.

"They plan to go farther than they have gone," Wyatt says.

"What?" Ada turns to him, distracted.

"*Ultravioleta*. They plan to leave the system. You know they will be trying to go somewhere that doesn't exist."

"They won't like it there," Ada says quietly.

"They will crash," Wyatt comments.

"Crash and burn," Ada stares at Stella's empty chair. "But why?" she looks fully at Wyatt.

"I don't know. Perhaps because he isn't me or you?" Wyatt says.

He seems courtly, hovering over Ada. She sees the hunter in him but doesn't care. She allows him to lead her away.

Finally only Marty is left at the table. He fingers his scarf and thinks of Elsie. He also thinks "Red," and says it aloud to himself. "Red," he goes on. The conjunction of Ada and Wyatt is as satisfying to him as the unlikely connection of Stella and Pontius.

"It's just like Earth, like Oakland in the old days," he says to himself. "Anyone with anyone."

Embarkation

When the light is right to leave it is unnecessary to spread the word. The passengers report as if for duty. Even Cap, having landed, is ready to go off on the expedition. He follows the guests as they gather at the paper atrium where they first entered the library. The mood is celebratory. Creamy Europan clouds like mountains seem to rise off the distant moon as the passengers saunter hand in hand, as in a country dance. The masts of the *Ultravioleta* are festooned with paper. The newly lined decks creak under the combined weight of passengers, crew and vast emotional baggage. The I among them seem to float as usual. There is a pink glow and an earthy edge to the buff of *Ultravioleta*'s stretched vellum. Something is falling like dust or down.

"Is it interstellar?" Nahid asks of the strange confetti as it settles around them. "Or perhaps dark matter?" She lifts the pale corner of her paper robe as she seems to fall forward in the dance.

"It feels like silk," Robinson says, helping her across an apparent void, feeling his hands circle her tiny waist. "Like a light rose satin or like…"

"The forms," she interrupts him, twisting away, pointing to what now seem like stars falling, "are different but alike, like what are those called?"

"Snowflakes?" he responds. "Or maybe it's fakes or aches. I can't quite remember, let's see, 'slakes,' that's it. We are slaked. Slakéd."

"But the mountains," Nahid turns to them. "There is water under the mountains and you can see everything in it and also through to the bottom."

"I see that, yes, to the bottom of the lake. There is something down there like a festival or a show of hands, a clapping or fluttering. Are those … what are they called? Fish, butterflies, lichen? French fries? Little fingers of something bright, they…"

Pontius approaches, urging them forward. He has a light touch as he herds what he thinks of as his little flock. They feel pushed as if by tiny hands, though Pontius' reach extends well beyond them. Cap floats by grinning maniacally. The remaining passengers drift onto *Ultravioleta*. There is a softness, a musicality, to the air, as they pour over the lip of the ship and enter something like a ballroom. There is a singing in their hearts but it is ultimately silent on this ark and there is a warmth to this musical silence that is unlike the usual cacophony of the radio. Everyone is turned down. Some are turned off, so filled are they with the quiet thought of each next musical step.

Tinia appears alone, crisply turned out in an iridescent ensemble that highlights the darkness of her nature. Marty nods, acknowledging her thoughtful participation as a fellow pilot. He brings up the rear of the party, artist's staff in his hand, like the Master. He thinks of Whistler as he smoothes the golden corduroys he always wears and floofs his red scarf. With a colorist's appreciation of the luster of those arrayed before him, he encourages everyone to take their time boarding and mingling with each other. With a formalist's sensitivity to the arrangement, he watches as they come together and disengage, only to unite again in what seems like a contradance to the dance with which they began.

"Why have I never noticed the beauty of these creatures?" he asks himself, watching Nahid and Robinson circle each other. "What fine specimens they are. What a riot of colors they possess in their tiny outfits. What thoughts in their tiny heads."

"You ready, X?" Pontius calls.

"Yo!" Marty replies. "I am that."

He and Pontius create a vanishing point, a mutual perspective to focus the passengers with and into. Tinia concurs from her plane paper cabin. The middle distance beckons. A rosy glow obtains. Light closes in. Darkness descends. At the last moment Dayv jumps aboard from the already detached gangway. Marty and Pontius envelope him in their thoughts. Tinia glows.

The ship's wheel materializes in Pontius' steady hands. Marty takes up his positions, simultaneously dreaming on the deck and looking out from the top of the mast, theatrically streaming like a flag of himself. Already the past looms behind them. *Ultravioleta* is under way.

Last Chance

Wyatt returns to the life of his mind. He goes to what holds him. Being with Holliday is like being a gun in a holster, like a star on a chest. He knows what is next. He knows he will watch as the doctor watches him die.

"Another, Holliday?" The bartender smiles.

"Don't mind if I do," Doc muses. "Don't mind if I don't. It's all one. It's all here. Don't matter where. Now that I've given myself the chair." He moves to a table, taking his guitar.

"It's a long way to heaven," Doc rambles, staring into his drink, thinking of the stars, he rests the guitar in his lap. "So they say but what do they know?" He finishes the drink in one swallow, calls for more. He feels his heart in his chest like any bird trying to escape from its nest. He relights his little cigar. The air in his lungs is perfectly still. It gets darker.

"Any time now." He thinks of Wyatt, of their life together. He feels the presence of his lover. The stars, the bars, the miles between. He fingers his badge. Plays a note. "Been meaning to say a thing or two to you, my dear." Doc falls back on his training. Turning away, he executes a perfect chord change. Always an aristocrat of the manly spirit, Doc is alive but dead, dying but dreaming, meaning but innocent of ever having meant anything.

"The world is made of thought," he says to himself. "I mean nothing. Nothing like desire. I mean need. Me. I mean I need the world like I need … what I mean is that nothing is made of desire but the world. Like a hole in the head."

Doc contemplates the fate of being a mere human mired in time. He takes out his gun.

"I wouldn't mind being left behind to represent the government, if it weren't so boring," he complains, knowing that Wyatt can hear him wherever he is or, which is the same thing, that they will repeat their comments to each other when they meet. Doc knows what Wyatt will say and what he will reply. Their conversations are written in stone in that sense but in another are always unwritten. Looking forward to not speaking to Wyatt is one of the real pleasures left to the good dentist, dying quietly as he is in the Last Chance Bar. In Tombstone. In the world. He strums a waltz, sings tunelessly.

This Nothing

Not as one feels but as
Remembered, remember?
That we can act

Potent, impossible and
Unspoken the unsaid (between us)
There is no agreement

No wind breathed
The book, the stars
All our space in one try

Our ship wrecks
The vanity of chance
The fate of this

"… unchanged neutrality of the abyss"
Too late (my love) to change
Anything we wish

We come to know
The goal of a mind whose will it is
For anything at all

To break breaks
The vessel opens (falls through)
"The shell of the self-evident"

An empty shell
A steady light
Divided from

"Entering him is like reading a lighted room," Doc muses. He is beginning to fray at the edges, to curl like a daguerreotype. He loads his gun. "If wishes were horses," he goes on, putting the gun aside, plucking a few more notes. He wants to think of Wyatt but someone else comes into his mind. An unfamiliar voice, an unknown face. A Mexican.

"He's gone," Marty says in Holliday's head. Doc opens his eyes wide into the impenetrable blue smoke of the room. He forms the word "No" with his mouth, silently, saying also "Why?" He sits up straight realizing, "Why not?" closing his eyes. He sets aside his guitar, picking up the gun. "This nothing," he sings.

Wyatt appears like lips above the horizon saying, "I'm not gone," but he knows it's too late.

It is a hot summer day. The birds are full of sky.

After You

"After you," Stella telegraphs to Wyatt. He sees the words of her particular penmanship ink themselves across his paper screen. "It is as if she is drawing my heart," he thinks though he knows himself to be heartless.

They have managed not to be together at the library hotel, in spite of the unusual situation of their being at the same place at the same time. Stella has contrived to be with Pontius. Wyatt, alone, has spent his days traveling through his various lives. As they leave The Gutenberg separately, Stella in the *Nautilus*, Wyatt in the *Stella*, they watch as *Ultravioleta* rocks angelically, far below. They see her filling with passengers who seem to waltz away from the library, as if they had not a care in the world.

"After all is said and done, there is nothing — nothing to win, nothing is won," Stella reflects, accelerating into the darkness, thinking again about the war, all of the wars. She is not sure if it is the many wars on Mars she considers so much as hers with Wyatt — only personal, not as horrible, and yet more ongoing, more inescapable.

The usual problem of the separation of wills is apparent as they leave the library behind for this meeting in space. It is their way. Wyatt with himself. Wyatt with Stella. He feels her flying. It seems like moments ago they were at the table. "I could have touched her, if this were a universe where such a gesture was conceivable. But I must lay aside the conceivable," he thinks, "to concentrate on what is already conceived." Wyatt has a bit of business on his mind. "The end of the world as we know it," he thinks. "Or at least as you do." He gazes out into space trying to find Stella who has slipped away again as usual.

Wyatt begins to blur as time catches up with him. Stella can feel it as she flees from him. Finally, he catches up with her. The taste of her, of them both, comes to him and he feels distracted by something. A human might call it love but to an I it is pure hunger. Sensing another chance, Stella flies away. "Away" is her only idea, though typically, she has sought the danger of this convocation. She feels caught in Wyatt's presence, in the fibres of his nerves, in his pages, his names, his musculature. The nomenclature of the I science of possession reads itself to her.

"I to you am simply I," he thinks. "But you are I, too, the mistress of…no the mother of the child of my eyes."

For a moment Stella doesn't feel him, or anything, and then she does again. The heady moment of his absence is with her as she finds the signal of him.

"I have no idea what you are talking about. You know, English is your first language, biographically speaking —"

"Bio, yes, that is what I wanted to get to. Our child —"

"Our what?" Stella stops in thought and in real space she stops, almost colliding with Wyatt.

"I had him with my eyes, as we do. I thought you would know, knew, but then I realized that you can't or hadn't… Remember when we… When you were my…"

"That was on another planet, man, a million years ago. You can't be telling me… Holy shit."

"It's funny, he often says just that when…"

"Right. When? When exactly?"

"Let's see. For me, you know, time is…"

"Jesus." Stella pulls away. Again she feels the discontinuity of Wyatt. The end of him appears like a final line, allowing her to think out into limitless space.

"A kid?" She has to say it.

"Well no…or yes, but not a child, though he is young. He came out that way. It was something about your smile I think. It gave him a quality of…"

"Where is he? Who is…"

"Oh, it's Dayv. I keep forgetting that you… He is very like… He takes after you, my love."

"Ah." The cosmos seems to expand for Stella, as if rooms and doors were opening up in her mind. She sees now that Dayv is the inevitable child. For the first time in a long time Stella begins to feel something inside her like a satisfied mind. "Only ever with Ada…," she begins. "This explains a lot," she goes on to herself. She considers the intimations, begins to see it as obvious in retrospect. She floats happily in the closure of knowing. "Dayv." She sees his round head and weird, bright eyes as if from inside of her own. Her momentary softness gives Wyatt his chance.

"Tom! no what...stop!" Stella flinches, trying to twist physically away though she is still alone. She finds Wyatt in more than her head. He is too familiar, too close, closer and thicker inside her than can be born. It is Wyatt, unborn, unknown. "I," he starts in on her and suddenly she knows with Wyatt what it is not to be real, all presence but not present. She senses his hideous need, feels him materialize like flesh inside her head and her heart. She feels possessed by his outrageous familiarity. It is as if his mind were his cock. Wyatt, as his old implacable self, enters her like a door.

"Who are you to... No... No! I know a thief when I see one. I can't let this happen again," she screams, trying to find a rhetoric that will play him. "How killed can I be before I am actually dead? What about the government? The question of government is not superceded by this one of family. Your simpleminded familiarity... Not this time. You have tried this with me before, asshole. Not that I don't believe you, but who is this 'we' you are proposing? It is never not you."

Stella feels compromised, conjugated, stymied, stalemated, but also that she can get away. With an effort she sees Wyatt, sees into him and finally through him, almost through — into his *approximate organs,* plainly visible now in their craven need to be...what? She sees him imagine himself to be her beloved enemy. Father but not faithful. Presence but not present. Paid but not paying. Pain. She sees him then for what he is — just a pure pain in the ass. Sees all the way through him, his need to be believed in. Finally, she replaces him with space. She believes in nothing.

Or anything. She goes on. Is somewhere, someone else.

"When I have ceased to be," Wyatt tries, momentarily ceasing to be. Stella reads him all over her like a tattoo, like a bruise or a scar. One last time. Last lines.

"Everything was always true between us, but it was never enough to keep us in the same place at the same time, even for a moment," she says.

Rapier-like, she sheaths herself, gone now, flown. Alone.

"It is rough in space," she thinks, thinking herself along with an almost inhuman burst of speed. "There are no points of view. No places to stop or stand. Always in flight with or around."

The lack of the sound of him echoes in her head. She is bruised inside and out.

"Dayv," she thinks and then thinks again fondly, "Dayv."

Wyatt writes, he writhes in space, seeing his fate laid out for him like a puzzle he wishes he had left unsolved.

Shipwrecked

Ultravioleta lists.

Characters are disarranged and conscripted into a travesty of thought. They become illegible to themselves. "One result is the fall through the literal world, the other, the fall by false interpretation," Ada reads. She reads the many texts that appear on her screen, first as a kind of writing in space, then as anomalous testimonies scrawled in light. Ada sees that the messages are passionate, desperate and philosophical. She realizes that they are from personal letters, that the paper of *Ultravioleta* has come from letters.

"That devil," she says to Dayv. "Marty never said anything about the letters, but then he never talks so how could it come up?"

Together, they consider the silence of Marty, as Ada manipulates her paper screen. They watch the ship begin to fade in and out of time. They are transfixed by the spectacle, unable to believe that such a vast craft could fail.

"Holy shit," Days says. "They are personal. They read like love letters. What was he thinking?"

"He used them to get more distance. It was a dangerous move. Ah, it's Tinia, but what is she doing?" Ada zeroes in on Tinia who acknowledges the connection, peering directly into their eyes for a moment from the screen, but then looks away, holding her hands over her ears.

"What is it they used to say?" Dayv says. "Unsinkable? The flight plan alone is like an encyclopedia. Is it the time storm? Why is she holding her head like that?"

"I don't know. They seem too confused to notice the storm. It's more like an analogic allegory rift. Never seen one before. I thought it was just a legend. Come to think of it, it is a legend but it clearly doesn't matter. Where is she going?"

"It's like the ship of idiots." Dayv looks worried. "Couple of the boys on board and my...and Tinia, but why is she running?"

"Fools," Ada says. "It's the ship of fools. Pontius is an adequate pilot and a voracious predator but I am not sure that will help him this time around. I thought Tinia might be able to affect the trajectory but something is wrong — and where the hell is Marty?"

"Look, she has fallen," Dayv says, finding Tinia again. He is mesmerized by the image of his lover and by the strange sound that has begun to drift from the screen.

"There is too much sound," Ada realizes, her hands flying over the console. "Or it's unsound. I can't tell, but it's too much. It's too high. Too high and too fast for them and for us."

Ada and Dayv stand back. There is a roar, a loss of connection and then a blank page.

On *Ultravioleta*, Tinia feels the interruption. She runs, leaving Pontius alone with the wheel. She feels the sound surround Pontius on the bridge. She finds that she is visualizing the sound in sync with the other passengers, mostly Robinsons. The sound seems like a living thing. They can actually see it leak into space where it pools and eddies before surging back into the ship through the portholes and through their own eyes — or so they believe. As the active ingredient of thought travel, their belief weighs them down at this crucial time, ripping through their concentrations, opening out into dangerous nothing.

The level of dissonance makes any sort of thought difficult, let alone getting anywhere with one's thoughts. Pontius is equivocal at the ship's wheel, perceiving the threat to the passengers and ship as a potential benefit to himself.

"A little human panic, wild running around — might be okay. Could be good," he muses as the wheel whirls through his monstrous hands. Pontius is driven by a sense of something like competence on the job to keep things afloat. It is as if he feels the inner pull of the old bureaucrat to produce results, though it is millennia since there has been anyone for him to answer to, even allowing that he was ever inclined to respond to a question. Marty, caught in the looped memories of his human divorce, is no help. He might even be the source of this wave of incomprehensibility.

"Elsie, Elsie," Pontius thinks he hears Marty call to his lost wife. But what Marty has lost is heaven. "*Ciel, ciel…*" he moans, darkening and becoming increasingly immobile in a far corner of the ship.

Reconnecting, Ada sees Marty cowering but she can't tell where she is in relation to the others. She looks for Nahid.

With the sensitivity of the vulnerable, Nahid has begun to respond to the signs of decay. Ada is able to pick up a faint image of her. The effects of the storm have entered Nahid like a test for something deadly. Ada perceives that time itself has become toxic. Alone on her cot, Nahid feels out of time. She feels audited. It is not an unfamiliar feeling. Consciousness, most of it not her own, seems to spill out of and around her. She feels sloppy with it. Paper rips. The origami of her world and heart opens out, flattening, tearing, dissolving. Everything she pictures is true already. Truth after truth terrifies her.

"Silence is golden," comes into her head meaninglessly and then something about loose lips. But she feels she can't be silent. She sees the myriad gilded edges of intimate letters flap from the walls and detach from the floor. Everything is in movement.

"I don't know why they call it stationary," she says. She finds she wants to speak, to chat, and scheme, to read the impassioned pleas and revealing claims in the endless missives she sees all around her.

Ada sees that the sound hasn't yet reached Nahid. Instead there is an eerie quiet filled with too much thought — with the ends of letters, the salutations, excuses, musings and insistences, the closings with love, the x's and o's in infinite rows.

"I wish I had a woman to talk to," Nahid mutters, noting to herself that she is speaking aloud. It occurs to her that the only woman here is Robinson but she knows this is wrong. Though possibly womanish in his emotional availability, Robinson is, one must admit, a man. His forms of communication as they are directed at herself have tended to be more manly, in fact, than she feels is called for at the moment. Her mind aches in puzzlement.

"But what the hell," she mumbles, her eyes like gigantic spots seem to suck in everything around her. "Any port in a…"

"Quite a little blow we are having here, darling." Robinson lumbers in as if she has willed him to her. "No action but in things," he begins. "Your eyes are the color of space."

Framed in the porthole on the papier mâché cot, they look out together at the loud darkness. They don't wait. They take each other apart.

"It's like the exit row here," Robinson says later, appreciatively. "I think we can easily escape." Nahid rests in his comfortingly human arms. She remembers thinking earlier that in fact there was no escape, but was that from Robinson? She can't remember now. It seems important but she can't get there. No one seems to be getting anywhere. That was the thing.

Nahid begins to fall into what she hopes is sleep with the word "Where" on her lips which are now bitten into an intense red. "Where will we be when we are gone," she manages to say though she is now almost fully sleeping.

Robinson considers recent events. Nahid is a great kid but he tells himself she lacks substance. "You feel alone in the dark," he complains to himself. "Well, alone with some great lips and eyes," he relents.

If the problem with Nahid is that she poses the terms but doesn't stay to argue them, the problem with Robinson, and Robinson knows this, is that he argues everything.

"We are not going down," he maintains, though the fact that he has said it aloud worries him. "I wonder where we are not going down to," he tries to think it through. He watches Nahid dream, believing himself to be in love. He gazes into the world of her slightly open mouth, thinking of his absent consort somewhere in the cosmos. He considers the possibility of M returning and jealously blasting the two of them into cinders. At this moment it would seem like a rescue.

"Very little likelihood of us ever being found, even by herself," he says as if in answer to a question. "We are fucked," he goes on, affectionately and, again, as if in a response to a detailed bit of reasoning on Nahid's part about the situation being dire and there being no exit in any sense.

"You've got me there. Here. I have to say I feel a bit insubstantial myself. Might catch a little shuteye, might rest some before…what is it they say? *The Gutenberg Gallaxy* or what is it?" He struggles with the hotel jingle. "We get it to you, you get… I always forget what you get."

Pontius appears abruptly, overfilling the door, arms outstretched like an enormous bird of prey. Believing he is a nightmare, Robinson ignores him. Pontius' mouth moves silently but then the roar starts, sounding to the humans like a machine, Robinson thinks it used to be called a jet. This behavior supports the nightmare idea. Robinson slips closer to Nahid, cradling her. Pontius roars again.

"Hey, you are waking the lady," Robinson says, trying to restrain

Nahid who gesticulates wildly. "Don't you guys call that something – subjective or…"

"Subjunctive," Pontius tries not to roar. He attempts to reconjugate laboriously, remaining somewhat breathless. "But, no, this is not that. It's very like but no, here everyone is out of sync. What are you doing merely fucking in here when we are…"

"Fucked?" Robinson chuckles. "But when are we not fucked, man – I mean given the situation on Mars and going back to the Imperatives…"

"Robinson, we are going down. Try to focus." But Pontius begins to blur as he speaks, looking into his hands, he covers his face. Hideously, they can see his face through his hands. He begins to roar again.

"Are you washed in the blood of the lamb? I hear a voice calling."

"Jesus, P." Nahid gets up, trying to smooth and rearrange herself. "Not more of that."

Robinson reaches for her but she pulls away from him. Together they watch Pontius fade in and out of view. Nahid edges toward the door.

"This is no time for technical difficulties." She looks down at her own hands. "I always said they were just broadcasts."

"I am not a broadcast, I am a station, a channel. I am media itself." Pontius is hopelessly distorted now like old modernism. He struggles to maintain his dignity or command or the sense among the passengers that he exists at all.

"It always comes to that with them," Ada thinks, watching from her distant perch. "That they exist. That is their whole claim."

Pontius freezes. He melts, moaning. He refreezes. The shipwide roar becomes an hysterical muttering and settles into a series of whoops and screams with a strange reverb that makes it seem almost cheerful.

"They're a ballsy group," Dayv comments, still watching from behind Ada. "They're trying to stay together like a chorus of harmonic thought — to hear and adhere to themselves."

"We are all we have." He hears them think. "Oh the humanity!" someone quotes. "We are going down!" someone else repeats, running past. They all seem to be Robinson, except Nahid, who pauses trying to discern her own voice in the screams but she is on her way away.

"No we are not!" Robinson thinks, watching himself run by. "We are not going down." He finds he is in unison with someone with this thought. He suspects it to be one of his selves but looks around for a possible accomplice.

"Baby, was that you?" He watches Nahid's black hair stream electrically behind her as she closes the hatch. He knows it was not. "The color of space," he thinks with some regret, remembering her eyes. He feels sleepy again.

Tinia walks in suited up in a red Mary jacket. "So it was you." Robinson gazes at her from what seems to him the endless length of himself. He feels that he can't quite wake up, that he has slipped again into a dream. Tinia sees herself in his dream but feels she can work inside it. "Done it many times," she thinks, taking a piece of paper from the hull fraying around them. Getting out her tea she rolls a cigarette. She exhales as she reads aloud from one of the endless texts around them.

"Dearest. My life ends each time I think of you. Here alone in the desert of what is not our life together I never speak except to sigh your name, your many names. My head fills with my heart. I am inside out, even as I work the livelong…"

"Stop. You're killing me…." But Robinson and Tinia have begun to make the ship with their breathing, their thinking. A critical but open attitude of heightened awareness tempered with fear is drawing them together.

Tinia takes another drag and, by exhaling, casts spectrums of thought around them like confetti in a parade. She breathes in and her thinking takes the form of a drawing of rain. Again she exhales and a polarized vapor of regret or grief appears. Livid densities of coherence congeal around her like mental weather. For the moment, she draws herself and Robinson together.

"Oh, baby," he starts but she keeps her distance, locking him into her pattern of brainy physicality.

"Hold on there, cowboy. Let's take a walk."

"*Ultravioleta*," they both say in a kind of round as they walk and breath. "*Ultra*," breathing in, "*Violeta*," breathing out. Eyes closed, they hold the ship in their minds, passing through ripped doors and torn walls, they see passengers, mostly other Robinsons, fainting, sleeping, falling into various stages of disrememberment, as it is terrifyingly called.

"We need to find Pontius." Tinia pulls her Mary leather around her, padding her pockets for more tea. "Bad as that might seem as an idea. Where are the goddamn boys when you need them?"

She lights up again. Pontius materializes. He tries to isolate himself with Tinia in a typically vicious circle but she easily breaks free and recontextualizes them all in something like a performance piece. The walls around them melt in icy flames as they head for the bridge. They arrive back in the big room, out of breath, almost out of life, and collapse. Exhausted, they sit together facing into themselves in an effort to exert control over their minds, their ship and their destinies. Tinia becomes aware of Dayv hovering, insistently in the background of her mind.

"I told you not to call me here. I am having a shipwreck!" Tinia snaps. "If you have to hang around, go find Marty." She continues to smile distractedly, cigarette hanging from her red mouth, eyes squinting against the smoke. Tinia concentrates as if she were throwing her voice but it is her thoughts she is projecting around the others as far and as fast as she humanly can.

"*Ultravioleta* is the moment of interlocking trajectories," Pontius starts in. He feels he has brought them all here and is easing himself into his role as a pedant, his second favorite to that of ravening predator. "A trajectory, in this sense, is a journey including at least the distance of a pot to piss in. The senses are disarranged but this is more of a side than a primary effect. So far we are dealing mainly with the present. The past comes into play as an available information stream but you have to be able to limit the contamination."

He demonstrates the stream with his huge hands, holding them apart as if to support a skein of yarn. Tinia feels her mind bend as if she is becoming a figure of speech. She feels the effect of Pontius in her head as that of a password on a sentry. He continues, unrelenting.

"We inhabit the past or aspects of character associated with it. Your desires — by we I mean I — your days determine what identities rise to the surface of the miasmas of your little minds. It is an honor to be taken by us really and flying is well-known to be the safest..."

"Okay, Einstein, just back off. There is really nothing better than to be had for lunch by one of you guys and I want us to get together sometime soon and we can do that — but right now let's talk about the ship. We are sort of breaking apart here or maybe going down. I feel fuzzy all the time. Interrupted, intermittent and chaosified, but not in a good way. Do you feel that? Do you feel anything?"

"Well yes, we are going down in a sense. I mean that's sort of a given on a trip like this. I thought you knew. No? Well, my dear, travel is, of course, all about the vicissitudes. You can't expect everything to be like a walk in the park."

Tina darkens into speechless consternation, beginning to seize up like a single muscle in spasm. Dayv hears all this as, with an effort, he asserts himself. Fully present now, he touches Tinia's back protectively, but she shakes him off.

Dayv addresses Pontius silently at first and then in a barely audible version of an I whisper.

"Are you flying this thing or sinking it? Can you keep your thoughts straight for two pots in a row? Maybe you've been out here too long. Old fart like yourself. It's not the I, it's the you, man. You just haven't got it. Talk about going down, going down where?"

"That's the thing, my boy," Pontius warms to this exchange. The hybridity of Dayv is pleasantly dissonant. The neither fish nor fowl quality of the youth is proving to be a distraction from the already compelling context of the sinking ship.

"This is turning out to be a really good day," he thinks with the sense of official evil that is the aspect of his own identity he most enjoys. His historic guilt along with a natural viciousness and vague sense of empire make Pontius perfect for himself. He wonders where Marty wanders in the midst of the mere regret and despair that is his wont.

"We need to talk about the trajectories and the dimensions." He feels himself rising to the occasion. "The dimensions and the connectedness." He locks his hands together simultaneously pulling them apart. They seem to Tinia to stretch unnaturally.

"You know how you feel and see the dimensions?" This to Dayv. "More than the folks, I mean. You know what I mean when I say dimensions? Your point of view, the aspects and constructedness of things. Yes? Anyway these dimensions are close together. They exist at the same time and there is leakage. Everyone knows that."

He looks around for agreement. Robinson is very still. Tinia smokes moodily.

"So that's it. The leakage. Everything exists in the leakage. I mean we do. That's how we get from place to place or know that we are somewhere other than or in addition to where we were. Are. *We* know it and sometimes they know it, too. They *get* it or it gets them." Chuckling again. "It's a beautiful system. But there are, ah, interruptions. Of course. They are built in, so to speak. You feel it most when you travel, especially if you happen to, you know, crash. It's best when you are crashing, really. The farther you go, the more you get it but at the same time you forget because there is this flow phenomenon. That's the other part. And it is best not to be too obvious, to think about it together. I mean it's not so much what I am saying as that I am saying it."

He reaches for Tinia who pulls away at first but then puts her small stained hands into his weird by-now transparent appendages. Robinson reaches out also, as does Dayv, and they think and move together in something like a waltz or a séance. Pontius drones on.

"It's impossible to say it because speech itself is another trajectory which means of course that it is impossible not to say it because the infinite possibilities are self-fulfilling and inevitable. But going down and breaking apart are — is — only one outcome among... I mean I speak as we go along like this but do we want to keep going? The very question emphasizes the flow aspect. You can get some serious mileage from overcoming doubt even if you are wrong. I mean we think we are sinking and gloriously we are. But it doesn't matter."

"So we are sinking and flying at the same time." Dayv elaborates. "We are simultaneously lost and found. Foundering. It is the outcomes. The outcomes are infinite. Each moment can explode into them. But we are not — can we be conscious of any of it really? Is it different for you — I mean us? I don't think it is for me." He seems to peer inside his head as if looking for parallel universes.

"Jesus, Mary and Joseph. I have never heard such a load of horseshit." Tinia exhales a black cloud of disbelief. "Don't you see that it's working for him?" She directs herself at Robinson and Dayv. "Don't you see that speaking and feeding are the same for him? It's an old Roman thing. To orate. Surround and conquer. Consume and well consume."

She strikes another match but instead of lighting a cigarette she holds it to the wall which flares fantastically. There is something like an implosion. It is all very sudden and when the smoke clears she is gone.

"T!" Dayv tries to scream but finds that he is following her, as does Robinson. They move through the ship as if through nothing at all and in fact the walls have become so porous they feel they are floating through starry space. Robinson wonders if he has died or if they have finally gone down and this is down. The question makes him think of Nahid. "Where is that child?" he wonders and feels satisfied that he can still wonder something. He finds he can't tell where he is in the ship. He has a feeling of lost time.

"What just happened?" he wonders.

"I saved your sorry ass." Tinia floats forward, head-first, heading to the other end of the ship, looking for Marty. She almost collides with him as they all enter a huge chamber cluttered with books and paintings.

"*Afternoon in Piedmont,*" she says loudly, right into Marty's face. She is determined to reconnect with Marty. She grips his shoulders. Marty looks at Tinia with eyes so filled with space as to obliterate the vast room around them.

"Elsie leaves you but she takes you back when you're dying," she yells. "Remember? Think about dying. It was nice. I mean bad in a way but nice. Think of her sweet old face and the kid. What's her name?"

"Micaela," Marty replies still in a half swoon, "with an M like mine."

"So you are not going down in flames. It's not the damn divorce. You're dying in bed in Oakland. Things are great. Okay, you're in a little pain but Elsie is still beautiful and you're not bad yourself. All those paintings. The yellow hills and the distance. Think of distance."

"It's not the end of the world, Marty, or the end of the ship," Dayv tries to be helpful. "It's just a time storm. Either we are causing it by thinking about what can't be known — the parallels, you know, and the outcomes, or the storm is this information. Do you see what I mean. It's a sort of reversal of cause and effect."

Tinia and Marty are not listening. They are focused on each other. Mental heat and the magnetism of revery wave out from them. Tinia continues to focus on Marty and Marty on the universe.

They know Dayv is wrong but it doesn't matter.

They all hold each other again. Robinson brings in a tray of drinks and Nahid reappears. But then Pontius is back. He closes his predator eyes as he huddles together with his prey, taking his sharp breaths.

"Let's go home," he says and Marty joins in. They lock together reeling in a monstrous dance. The humans and Dayv hold on for dear life and it seems to them that *Ultravioleta* coheres for a moment in perfect space. Her portholes are lined up like eyes, her decks are smart, her paper crackles in the void.

They realize the huge room they are in is the bridge seen from another view. Their location has not changed only their perspective — or so they believe. Pontius and Marty walk away from each other. Marty begins moving things around in the room and the ship's wheel appears. Pontius takes it whistling. Marty reties his red scarf.

"We have saved her but for what?" Tinia thinks. "Where do we think we are going?"

"Away together," Dayv thinks back. Tinia nods. Robinson looks thoughtful. "We are already gone," he says.

Back on her cot, Nahid is odalisque with her ancient pen and a new notebook torn from the deck. She is in touch with the library. "Oh, Mama," she writes, thinking of Ada. She feels her experience of events to have been different from that of everyone else. She thinks she knows where they are going but believes that no one will believe her if she says it, so she writes it instead. She begins by quoting from the Gospel of Mary.

"Whence do you come, killer of humans, and where are you going, conqueror of space?"

Being Read

"That the monsters were present among us was clear from the start. The hunger of the I is well documented, that of Pontius is legendary. It is known to be a force of nature, if the I can be thought of as part of nature. But was it only Pontius? What has he done? What force beyond the time storm has taken us?"

Nahid closes her notebook, running her hands over the thick paper. She tries to piece together why they have gone down and where they have gone down to. Are they like the discarded shells of creatures or the skins of fruit — remnants of themselves? The only things left seem to be the words. The words are everywhere. Wondering if these words are their minds emptied out, Nahid finds she knows nothing about the words but to write them. Opening to a fresh page, she begins to write. She feels hypnotized as she works, the words seem to explain themselves as they pour out of her.

"Red not of the world or of the universe, not Martian red but the feeling of being read, as if the words were plucked out of our minds and returned bloody from their dark inking into consciousness. There is a feeling of being alive in a place where the idea of living rather than actually being alive is the paradigm. And where a gelatinous color not like blood, not animal but also not mineral, not Sol far away going down, but ourselves sinking into something pink, darkens until it is definitively, entirely red."

Ada reads as Nahid works. She knows that the return of her guests is imminent, though they seem not to know it. Nahid continues, her lovely dark brows knitted expressively as she allows her pen to run away with her.

"As *Ultravioletans*, we feel — we are, in fact — extensively read. The text comes alive in our heads. We are born along and born again (and again) into text. We are viewed, hued, taken up and let alone, let go. Hole after hole opens before us, making for a sense of movement and yet we feel we are not going but coming. That we are arrived into something. That we are consumed."

Ada sighs. Never has the simple fact of being eaten seemed so complicated. Worrying for her fellow Mary, Ada looks around for Tinia and finds her smoking in a corner of the vast red room. Somehow she has found a flask of tea.

"It's not as if we haven't been eaten before," Tinia comments, pocketing the flask. Heads turn in her direction, reminding the assembled company that they have heads and can turn them. She recognizes everyone, mentally counting them up. It is impossible to keep track of the Robinsons. Though she does not know where she is, where they all are, it is clear to Tinia that they have been, in some sense, swallowed.

"We aren't dead but we are out of time again. Further than… I mean we are also not back…not back before we left as sometimes happens. But we are…how to say…." Unable to continue, Tinia takes more tea. She finds it impossible to think. The only options are to write or to drink. Tinia drinks.

"Is this heaven?" Robinson wonders. "Have we saved ourselves? Where is Dayv?" He holds out his hands, palms up and begins to read what appears to be a prayer.

"I think not," Nahid interrupts. "Not exactly heaven. No." She reaches for his hands, holding them in her own. When she turns her hands up, she sees that they are also crawling with words. They watch fascinated as the two sets of text combine.

THE INSTANT I END TO END	ENDED BY NIGHT NOT
NOT PAIN AGAIN ALL ONE	TO ONE NOT ME NOT NAMED
NOT LEFT OFF WEARY LEAVES	WHY THE FALLEN SAME
AS NOT COME UNDONE	SOME ONE DAY NOT GONE I THE
TREES GROW WHAT ARE	THEY? THEN

The gap between the lines causes a dizziness in both reader and written on. Tinia and Robinson exchange looks.

"Where has this traveling by thought brought us?" one of them says, while the other looks on stunned. They are not sure who has spoken. Tinia looks down to find her own flesh contextualized. She hears herself reading aloud.

CAPITAL OF SPACE CATEGORY OF ONE ARRIVES WITH THIS AND NOT

CONSUMED BUT ORDERLY SEEKS PARADISE ALONE OF ALL GOALS

It is as if her eyes create each next word as she reads, as if she reads as she sleeps, or sleeps dreaming that she has been captured and eaten. She watches Nahid transcribing everything. Whatever Nahid writes is legible somewhere on Nahid. She is writing herself like a book. Inking her own letters, printing her own press.

"Absurd idea. We are our own instruments," Tinia hears herself think. "Help," she says quietly. "Fuck," she continues, in order to say rather than read something. She reaches for her flask. Ignoring the fact that the sweet green tea seems to swarm with words, she tips it into her mouth, swallowing hard. She feels herself go white like a sheet. Her body seems to descend from her neck like a waterfall of illustrated flesh. The words appearing as if projected there and now everywhere focus the sleepy attentions of everyone. They feel they are being read to sleep, or read to death.

"Is this what you want?" Pontius floats by, above the general distress, owning it. They all wonder if they are caught in his mind. Hideous thought.

"Marty?" Tinia wakes herself fully and gets to her feet thinking of Marty. It is only when she rises that she realizes she was prone. "It's either all over or we're almost home," she thinks.

Tinia runs and then walks feeling she is making no progress. She falls and then rises, falling again. When she falls still again she finds Marty. He is resting on a pile, a pedestal, of papers and books.

"Look, these are by me," he hands Tinia the largest of them, a huge volume with a drawing of clouds on it and lightning bolts that radiate out from its cover.

"But it's all in I," she says, staring at the blank pages.

Marty is like a statue of himself. The words in his head and those on the pages seem just out of reach, his *approximate organs* ache visibly. Tinia is transfixed by him, by them. She is bending uncomprehendingly over the pages of the book when Dayv, who has come to look for Tinia, finds her. He sees what she has done by locating Marty, though she has herself forgotten. "There is not much paper in this book," he thinks, "and less thought, but there is enough to travel for a least a stanza. Not enough to get back but it's a start."

Dayv realizes now that they will get out by going back. He is not sure if it is in time but feels it is not. Not quite. They will go backward in space while going forward in time. Apparently humans did that a lot. None of them seemed surprised by it. Or possibly they are too stunned to register the shock they feel. At least they can still read if not think. They can see the paper in front of their faces. In fact Nahid is quite ebullient, if one can judge from the stuff written on her forehead. He longs to be alone with Tinia. He feels he has pursued her across the known universe and she has barely noticed. He realizes that this makes her perfect for him and strategizes what he thinks of as her rescue. He feels them being sucked back to The Gutenberg. He considers everyday life in the library. "That is truly paradise," he says aloud, but he knows it is unlikely to seem so to the survivors.

When they return to The Gutenberg it is unclear to everyone that they have ever left, except that, unanimously, they feel they have. The bedraggled group of souls frays as Ada talks them in one by one. They plop down. They barely make it up the gangway. She seems unperturbed to see them back, but that is how she always seems. She directs them to freshly papered rooms. It was clear from the start that the expedition was too ambitious but something else is going on here. There is grumbling about a Case Barrier. Among the passengers it is felt that there is something missing. They believe it is themselves. Even as they return they feel more gone than ever.

"Watch your step as you descend," Ada says automatically. "You don't want to tear anything."

Pontius leers by. Marty makes his way to his studio, only slightly the worse for wear. The other passengers continue to feel not back. Not out of whatever they were in. In escaping physically they have become divided from themselves. The story of their emergency continues to be legible on each of them. They gasp for breath. They stand stock still trying to discern the meanings of what they are saying and hearing and reading. Thought, they feel, has betrayed them and they are still thinking.

"How did we get out?" Tinia asks. "How back? And what about now? How do we get out of this?" It is a human problem. Robinson feels he has been awake for days, years.

Nahid can't stop writing. When she stops the text in her notebook it spills out onto the paper walls and onto her skin again. She reads as she takes notes. Alone among the humans, she seems unconcerned. The displacement of the words feels expected to her now. The words seem to know her mind. They are indirect but she senses that there is a writer and that he has been in the kind of trouble she is in somewhere, sometime. Nahid anticipates the story, sensing that it will get them all the way back, though it is a story of not getting back. She feels herself writing as reading, of knowing more than she knows. She identifies in advance with the characters — with the falseness of the Astrologer and the cynicism of the Countess, her need to account for everything. Believing there is a unifying moment of coherence to be found in the text, Nahid looks forward to reading anxiously, breathlessly.

Robinson reads Nahid though he is profoundly tired of reading. Tinia refuses to read, begins to read and then stops. She lies back limply on the platform in the observatory, supported by Dayv, consciously willing herself to become part of the pattern of the old textiles they rest on there. Dayv can read her but he knows it is not his reading that will be useful. He knows she has to read. She has to read and right herself. Tinia reaches for Marty's book. Dayv has brought it to her. She holds it to her chest as if to shield herself from the other texts that continue to appear around them. Stories begin to form, characters to appear and she can't keep from knowing what they say.

"Who are these creatures to me?" she complains. "Mere characters, suggestions, like actors on the stage of the page. Why do I have to go with them? Am I not already nowhere?" But she accepts another book from Dayv. This one is a thick paper notebook. It is by Eddie Zed, known on Mars as Stendahl. Dayv observes the work in it to be more event than text. Eddie writes into the situation they are all in, addressing also the historic despair of his Martian predicament. Marty writes of nothing. The passengers write and read Marty's story but it doesn't get them back, if anything, makes them feel farther out, like Marty.

Finally they connect with Eddie's text. Nahid has already found it. The story takes them down and back. Like them, like him, it is live.

Logical Astrology

"How one gets out is typically occluded by how one got in. It is just a matter of reading the situation correctly. Reading into and then out of it," Eddie comments to himself, as much as to his readers. He observes the effect of his thoughts occurring to several minds at once. His writing appears on the walls near a woman and on the face of a person he realizes is not a human. He becomes aware of the I energy of Dayv, oddly compromised by human warmth. He turns back to Nahid. He finds that he is startled by her and that she is as open to him as he is to her. His writing migrates from her walls to her skin. He watches as she reads hungrily, her hair streaming out behind her like night. As the others read, Nahid begins to write. She is an aggressive reader. She takes over. She is full of something strange. After a while, he recognizes it as hope. Eddie and Nahid write together. They begin with a line she remembers from the human Blanchot:

"More decisive than the rending of worlds is the demand that rejects the very horizon of a world." Eddie sees these new words written in Nahid's mind, in her notebook and on her paper cot. They become his words, his thought. He watches entranced as she lies back reading him as if from inside her eyes.

Nahid notices of herself that she is no longer frantic. "Not killed by fear," she writes happily, carefully, thinking, "I am receiving you loud and clear." Eddie continues to write. Nahid writes. The others try to keep up. Finally they are all reading together. The story carries them along.

"There are no planets without people," the Astrologer begins. "No fortune unaccounted for. No change left to chance. It is all perception. The effect of conceiving the system determines the effectiveness of understanding it. My calculations indicate…."

The Countess looks into his eyes, recognizing the point about to be made. Hers is a mantra of watching, his of saying. She knows it is a charade but of what? He believes the chart he casts for her is a seduction. She is so far beyond that idea as to make it seem quaint. He recites the chart like a poem. His work is just rough enough to seem real. The lovely absurdity of his conceit of the real is relaxing, even almost convincing. The Countess is not seduced but caught in the discourse of seduction. The speaking of the thing exists just outside the ring of its being real. There she thrives. There she wonders what this could be about.

"I can feel Mars rolling backwards in your mind," she starts, but the Astrologer interrupts.

"The whole retrograde issue is passé. What could be more ridiculous than a planet changing direction? Even in a head like yours. Even in mine. Mars can't change any more than I can. We are driven by gravity and desire. Just like them…."

"But they are not," she feels she would be angry if she had the strength. "They are not alive."

"What you are saying is absurd. Haven't we learned anything? It is only the planets that are alive. We in our puny discontinuity can hardly claim life only for ourselves. It is them…it was Mars that…that rescued itself, during that last reign of fire and the waves of…of whatever that was. Those wars, those monsters, and revolutions, invasions, infiltrations, rabble rousings, espionage. They are all false biological responses to the desire to survive in an environment hostile to mere animal life. Mars has its own will of wind and billion year old ice…."

"But you are an animal. We are both animals or so it is said. And there is nothing inherently wrong with a false conclusion at which one has honorably arrived. The falsity of the atmosphere there, here," she looks out from their island in the Hourglass Sea, knowing it to be entirely contrived of memory. She is acutely aware that they occupy the daydream of text that is like a map of nothing. She wants to weep with the lies she perceives around her. It is hard to locate the falseness of the Astrologer. As he promulgates his philosophy of prevarication he is, of course, lying. A corollary to his hatred of animals is the coat he wears which consists entirely of representations of the beasts he claims to despise. That he finds himself despicable is less apparent but no less important as a fact in his case. The Astrologer is a grotesque. He is made of the pieces of things, the ejecta of his own mind. He is pieced together by a desire so twisted it fails to recognize itself when, on turning, it meets its own visage pretending to be or believe in something it is not.

"Desire for the next thing," he says, as if in response to her thought, "knowing what to want, is no small triumph for a person or certainly not for a simpleminded interlocutress like yourself."

"Ah, what a cheap little snake you are. I should have known and I did know. I warned myself but I didn't listen. You have gone too far in your fakery. Your whole equal and opposite stance, as if you had anything to stand on. You are a figment of your own past — overacting, overreacting to the situation which is and, as you know, has always been, imagined. Our predicament is the logical result of recent history and the inevitable resistance you have encountered to, let us call them, your charms. It was you, wounded, asleep, face down with that possession of one thing crossing into the other that all you astrologers fall for, who fell for my line...."

"I am determined not to know anything among you," the Astrologer draws himself up, falling back again, this time to an ancient text. He tries to avoid the diatribes of the Countess. He knows she knows but it doesn't help him. They look away. They begin to dissolve until one can see through them to the false map beneath. Illusion after illusion is peeled away as their two bodies separate from the scene. Their story is ending by having not ever existed, as they do not.

Eddie lays down his pen, steepling his perfect fingers. He can't go on. Minds detach from his like suckers leaving their imprint on him, all but one.

"I find myself burnt in paper," he thinks, "old paper in new leather. The feeling of being written there is to be better read than I have ever been. It is like skin to my skin. I am skinned."

Nahid rolls over on her back, considering her ceiling which looks for all the world like a painting of a heaven. She rhymes glory with story, up with down, out with doubt. She thinks of the influence of plants on minerals, of minerals on the sky. A corona of hair surrounds her mind. She curls around her paper notebook. A storm of questions forms inside her, taking the place of recent storms.

"No, I have never been to Mars," she responds to one of them. "But yes, I would like to come." She realizes that this is sex but textual. She and Eddie have already begun. The other humans are distracted by this delectable turn of events. Only Dayv notices that while they have been reading and sleeping and traveling back in thought, the monsters have taken over the library.

Pocket History of the Universe

The I are a site for themselves. The intense energy of their collective presence thins the glass of the library observatory to a membrane not unlike the scales of a fish or a cataract attached to an eye. The stars effervesce through this lens, but the inner light of the I is the main source of illumination here. The I swarm. They occupy The Gutenberg as if they were animals and it was a world made of air and earth. They sink into the paper decks, into each other, thickly, muddily, as into a vast swamp or garden. They are each all subject and no ground. Or they are all ground.

They have tea. They have each other for the asking. Nameless and borderless, they transgress and transpire, sip and sigh, mewing, musing, winding, whining and whispering in I. It is only the humans they occupy who perceive them as predators, as the pure force of hunger. To themselves they are something to be cultivated. To themselves they are just conversation.

Automatically, Ada presides. Dayv hovers at her side. She sees more I than she has ever seen, recognizing herself, for the first time, to be among the devils, as she would once have called them — a mere name among names, no longer human or even clone. She feels however that she might finally be home. This resistant, invasive, hostile universe is strangely sweet to her. Dayv feels at home because that is how he always feels. He observes Ada, fascinated by her dark brooding. The violet of her eyes seems to extend all around them. He can tell she is thinking of Wyatt.

"I was always only Ada, barely even Byron. I identify with everything, everyone and yet really nothing, no one. No one except Stella," she says, "but Stella is always only the past. She is like the light of the stars, seeming to be young and bright but is actually old before her time. She is my ex as you are hers."

Ada looks at Dayv but doesn't see him. She addresses Wyatt. He isn't really there yet he seems to exist. She tries to find him, though she knows that he survives only in her mind. She feels torn by the knowledge.

"Wyatt, you old I," she murmurs quaintly, remembering his old lines, quoting them. "You who change by seeing."

Ada refers not to Wyatt's own words but to an ancient text, fragments of which exist in the mind of every I who has had anything to do with Earth. It is called the *Pocket History of the Universe*. Valuing the allusive and digressive qualities, especially of the badly translated versions, the I consider it a central document. They quote and paraphrase freely from it when, as now, they are gathered together. There are copies in several human languages in the library and Ada sees finally why she felt compelled to acquire them, though the I apparently don't need to see them to read them.

"The cheap man, his humanity compromised, wins...," Pontius chimes in with a familiar phrase, adding with his usual hideous smile, his favorite line. "I win," he sings and then repeats, "I win."

"The flowers decompose," Marty quotes, taking the discussion down the usual associative spiral. Ada sees him roll by, his red scarf elongated like a streak in the sky.

"This world is younger than your math," she replies, watching as her fellow monsters fly around her head. She feels rather than hears an interjection coming from the other side of the observatory.

"Romantic anti-police seek innocent one." It's Wyatt. He makes his way toward her.

"Tom," Ada says when he is beside her, though she has never before used his Christian name.

"The reader will learn to consider doubt," she continues, as if reading his mind. She finds she is imagining Wyatt, though she sees him before her. She realizes also that she is thinking of his death and that she can't quite think of it.

"Strong and weak eat the force within each," she hears or did she say it?

"The second direction is dead," Wyatt says.

"Stop thinking me," Ada objects, "that you are I." But she knows he is, they are. They all are.

"Quiet communication, oval face, prehistoric eyebrows," Pontius comments. He is quickly growing larger than the environment, large even for an I.

"They are not," Ada snaps. "They are creatures with hearts just like ourselves," she adds, distractedly, "or they would be like us if we had hearts."

"Wyatt," she goes on, pursuing the inevitable direction of her own thoughts. Ada cries in I, mental tears clinging to her. She wonders why she feels so far outside what she used to think of as her mind and wonders further why this disassociation gives her such a strong sense of well-being.

"Are they tears of joy?" She hears the question inside her head.

"Being dead," she also hears, "yet speaketh I."

"As the substance of the thing hoped for," she observes, "is not the thing seen."

She feels Wyatt inside her now, in spite of everything.

"Between us, no one can know what I know. Groundless though I walk with you," Wyatt persists in Ada's mind.

"But is he alive?" she says aloud.

Pontius floats past again and she realizes she has thought of this creature as something growing when in fact he is actually dying back while he gets larger, like a star or like the remission of a sickness that is, however, already mortal.

"I miss him," she thinks this of Wyatt, though he is beside her in some sense. The pain of missing him makes her feel alive.

"But are we ever alive? Or are we a special effect, engineered, like the new caffeine?" she thinks bitterly. "Is physical presence proof of anything? Is it enough?"

"We are injured," Wyatt replies, finally fully present. "I believe injured is the word that applies to what I am and to what you are."

"As the substance of things hoped for slips away," Ada repeats, "is not the substance of the things seen. But I see you now. I see you know me."

"Expensive to walk with you. Groundless where I go alone," Wyatt observes, rattling around in Ada's mind and she wonders again if he is alive or if "alive" is a category of being that applies to anyone here.

"Me," Wyatt adds, materializing enough so that Ada feels that she can again see him.

"He is not in my head but at my table," she says to herself, reaching for the tea. The gilded blue pot shines like the core of the world they circle. Wyatt appears relaxed before her, resplendent in his black and white, bright as she has ever seen him.

"Are you resurrected or were you never dead?" Ada pours as he holds out a translucent cup.

"Typical Mary question," he replies. "You Marys are blessed with not knowing — or you should be. That you have minds at all is the problem. It's like a growth obscuring what should be your hearts."

Wyatt's old-fashioned misogyny is barely intelligible to Ada, though she values its engaged, anachronistic malevolence. She regards him fondly.

"You are like a telescope or a corridor down into time," she says more to herself than to him. "A root, a route, a tendril. You are like a dragon written into an old margin."

"Not down," he returns, "but out. On. Not long but long gone. I am not lying and am no more dragon than lion or any other scripted being, no more root than branch."

But Ada retains her old knowledge of Wyatt. She finds that seeing him alive, talking to him, even pouring his tea is not a cure for believing he is dead. He seems detached.

"We only go off," Marty comments, floating by, as if to corroborate her worst fears, "We go off for a while — it's not like dying."

"More like dancing than dying, a sort of final blow or final blowout," Dayv asserts, pouring tea for himself and Marty as they settle in to witness this exchange. They see that Ada has eyes only for Wyatt, yet they find themselves basking in the fantastic purple waves of her vision.

"I am not blessed and I know everything." Ada resumes her scrutiny of her old lover. "Or at least I know that I am I and that you are dead or that you are the death of someone else — another I. Another I will die."

Ada feels she is alone in the cosmos with Wyatt. She finds that being filled with him has made her want Stella in her mind as a protection or antidote, but Ada can't find Stella. She gropes mentally, frantically in I and finds someone, something else — the nameless female presence, Mary, Messalina, Medea — as if she,

M, was lying in wait the whole time, as if she was a reflection in the muddy pool of time or in Ada's own untouched cup of tea.

"Even as I, this one is female," Ada thinks, reveling in what seems like the vestige of her old clonish identity as despised other. "The decomposition of flowers," she anomalously thinks, falling back on the sacred text. The decomposition of flowers is the way she finds into the mind of the entity she now realizes is her counterpart.

"The lotus in the pond," M sighs as Ada attempts to think it through. "The second life, the second I."

"The second I see you," Wyatt extemporizes.

"He is alive," M and Ada say as if Wyatt weren't there and as if they were actually saying he had died.

Dreaming together they enter a forest or into the idea of trees. Ada looks for trees but finds only seeds and flowers smashed like atoms into very moist ground. She sees pools with flowers floating in them. She wonders if it is only the "mirror of language," as in the *Pocket History* or if they have really entered a realm that constitutes a romantic whole.

"Let me go," they think together. It is the motto of the robots but it doesn't work for them. They can't let go any more than they can stay together.

"Do I get a say?" Wyatt asks, effectively and suddenly, ending the illusion or the allusion.

M hovers, matching her stars to the stars, she says, "You get whatever you want. It's your party."

"Why is what I want and being nought always the same thing? Is it so only in my mind, only true in this life?" Wyatt says, looking back on his various lives.

"I think it's the government," Ada responds, receding into her old self, applying her old logic as she remembers the real source of malevolence in the universe. At this thought Pontius reconstitutes terrifyingly near. As I, Ada theoretically has no need to fear him, but she does. He seems brutal as he appears in the full regalia of his official position. He is not smiling now.

"Or a say is all you get and then it's over. Or it's not over but it changes. It is unrecognizable. It dies when you die. But you have to go through it to do it. Before you rest you have to take every step. People forget that about dying," Ada adds.

"The steps, yes, until I rest. I get it. I get to take them. Until I am clear." Wyatt becomes what he fears, fading again into non-existence.

Ada closes her eyes. If she was able to sleep she would fall asleep now. As it is she dreams methodically of the lotus, starting with its reflection. The pond spreads out in her mind. She watches inwardly as she allows the bright flower to shine through her skin.

Dayv lingers in the background with Marty.

"Where will you go?" Dayv regards Marty as if he were already gone.

"It's not so much where I'll go as where I'll be," Marty replies, "When it all falls out. I can think of a few colors I need to follow up on. There is a kind of darkness I haven't gotten to before that I think I might get to now."

"A forest?" Dayv asks.

"More of a room than a forest," Marty pictures it. "I'll be in a room in a life."

"I see it now, yes. You are right. Me too," Dayv responds, thinking of the records that will be made, of the infinite principles of organization that will need to be applied.

He looks down at the odalisque of Ada, her violet eyes shut like a light. The nameless female presence is present but understated, like a dark veil.

"I'll be here in the library," Dayv says, gathering the tea things onto an enormous silver tray that reflects the worlds whirling around them. "I'll just straighten up here and then I'll work out the new categories — Death of the I, The Return, The New Rules. There's a lot of work to do."

"But how will people get here?" Marty wonders. "Will we be able to return?"

"What do you mean 'we'?" Dayv says as if from a great distance. He has already moved on. He recedes like a vanishing point, separating himself from Marty and from the other I. It occurs to him that they might be dying but he doesn't care. He hefts his tray, balancing it like a waiter at the end of his day. Moving off, he seems almost to dance down the sight lines remaining in the observatory from the infestation of I, there and in the universe, which is beginning to end. The first person view the I have had from the big bang down to the present seems to remain as a pattern of thought or a problem, but only Dayv knows.

"The rules have changed," he thinks. "It is the least one can say of what is left. And having discerned these new rules, what can one do but follow them?"

Many Worlds (Theory)

The observatory bulges out into space, I-less now, except for Ada, hidden in her chamber, which hangs above it like a box over a stage. Tinia wanders in, books and notebook in hand, and finds a place to stretch out among the rich textiles heaped up against the glass and paper walls of the room. She wants to read, write and observe, as is, it occurs to her, appropriate in the observatory. Lately, it is her only refuge. Tinia rests there in and among the rugs.

"These textiles can be read, as well as appreciated for their tactile qualities. People used to fly them," she writes into the thick paper of her notebook. "Gravity — or the love of heavenly bodies for each other," she continues, "is closer to human love than thought."

She wants to get to the theory of the many worlds. She feels them inside and around her. What she thinks of as the practice of the many worlds seems long and active to her but she wants to read something about it, or write it. In the realm of thought, Tinia is all action but she is tired of action now. She wants to think without acting. She wants to think and write.

"The many worlds are known to be parallel to the parallel universes first postulated centuries ago to explain the leakages between them," she reads, wondering if it is the universes or worlds that leaked. Her experience has included both. She reviews the article open before her, strangely inert in the ink of its old style printing. Finally, she begins to compose a series of statements about the worlds.

"The many worlds are effectively infinite but only so many exist at one time as can be known," she begins.

She stops to roll a cigarette wondering if it is appropriate to be obvious. Deciding that it is, she continues.

"All worlds are inhabited. Every world contains within it the inevitable death of its inhabitants."

"Worlds are comprised of various elements, not all of them solid or even discernable."

This idea chimes with Tinia's recent experience. She lies back, taking a long drag of tea. She is meditative, iridescent, the patterns on her skin glow like those of the rugs around her. Tinia curls around her notebook, writing awkwardly.

"Worlds are permeable, temporary, reachable, inhabited, vast, common and false."

Bringing herself up from a prone position, Tinia looks out at the lights of the many worlds, feeling an overwhelming sense of sadness and desire.

"War exists among the worlds," she goes on as if in response to a kind of dictation. She doesn't think it is the I but then she thinks it might be and focuses herself inwardly, trying to locate the familiar signs but she decides it is not them but her own thought. She finds she is not invaded and that the only inner event worth noting is that she is bleeding. The proximity of Jupiter's four moons, so distracting in their multiplicity, complicate the menses, but she doesn't mind. She continues to sip the tea in her cup and to smoke the tea in her cigarette, feeling the consequent regulation of her inner humors work itself out. She narrows her eyes, reading. The moons and planets seem to dance around the library. She feels them intersect right at the point of her life.

When Dayv appears her she envelops him in her thoughts. They are quiet for awhile but soon they are wound together like a knot. Previously Dayv's sex has made her think of the yellow of ivory but now its white round head seems like a moon, she is not sure which one. Dayv feels real to Tinia in a universe where even the many worlds are questionable. To Dayv, Tinia is the many worlds. As I, her cries are more nourishing to him than any feast. As human, her patterns feel more familiar to him than his own skin.

When Tinia is quiet again and Dayv has gone off, she sits back, bleeding and thinking, smoking. The smoke sweetens the air in her vicinity, taking the shapes of her thoughts. She has a theory about the Case Barrier, about the many worlds. Something about pattern, not a specific pattern but pattern as an idea. Things that are a copy of the mind of the viewer when the viewer's mind rises up.

She closes her eyes around her thinking, trying to get to it. She opens them when she hears Stella climb up into Ada's room. "Against gravity," Tinia thinks, watching her enter Ada's chamber where they are framed by the big window of the room. Stella and Ada circle each other like two Juliets. It is as if they are both brides. Waves ripple like crinolines around them. The waves feel like time. Compelling as it is at first, Tinia finally forgets to watch this little melodrama. She resumes her reading of the worlds, the moons, the scroll in her hands and the ones in her head.

When she hears a cry she looks up, seeing Stella leave the chamber. Stella descends into the observatory in a rustling of raw golden energy. Thought pours off her like sweat. She glistens in her transparence, collapsing beside Tinia, who is darkly coiled as usual. Stella takes the bag of tea, crumbling it into a piece of paper. She runs the paper along her tongue, twisting the edges absently. She hands it to Tinia and repeats the process. Tinia lights her own tea and that of Stella who retrieves a leaf from her mouth and she inhales deeply. They smoke and look out at Ganymede.

"She is not really one of us," Stella says. "I mean she is, but she's not. She is one of us but she is not real."

"But she's a Mary and she…on Mars…I mean, clones are just…"

"She's a Mary yes but she's not a clone. Never was. I see it now. Nothing is ever what it is for us. Or at least for me. Maybe it's just that I'm not real."

"Are we real or are we here at all?" Tinia wonders aloud, thinking Stella might actually know. It is the usual question. She has forgotten to watch the moons but now she looks up at them, trying to get away from Stella and back into her own thinking, but Stella draws her in.

"Beats the hell out of me. Listen!"

"She is crying." Tinia is alarmed. It is unthinkable that Ada would allow herself to cry. Tinia peers up into the overhanging room, but sees nothing.

"Not that," Stella says. "There's another sound. It's like a massive humming as if it was from…. Come on. I know what it is. I think it's the horizon sinking into the Case Barrier or vice versa. I know it is. Let's go."

As Tinia follows Stella, she sees the moons through the paper wall before them and through the paper door as they tear through it. Europa, very close now, looms. Its giant shadow darkens the room.

Stella has willed Tinia onto the *Nautilus*. Tinia tries to escape but before she can get out, the tiny ship closes over them. It has already begun to rise.

"Oh no," Tinia complains quietly. "So much for thought," she thinks. She feels something curling up inside her, caught among the traces of Dayv and her own blood. "Blood of the stars," she murmurs, but it is not stars she perceives.

"Plants," she says, sleepy now. She feels the velocity as Stella pours it on. "Ants or creatures or patterns…Stella…," she moans. The sleepiness of unprepared thought travel brings her back to the recent storms, the attacks. She dreams she is on Mars and can't wake up or sleep. "No!" she says again.

"Not crying," Stella murmurs. "She was not crying but singing in I. She is I."

"But I am not I, damn it. Slow this thing…. What are you saying? Is she…is it the government? Isn't she the government? And that sound — is it radio? Yes, that's what it is. That must be it. Natural radio. I've heard of this. It's spheroids or something. What is it that Dayv says, 'music of the balls?' The heavenly bodies themselves broadcast and make this…. It's a high discontinuity, a sort of peeping or seepage into space."

"Not spheroids, spherics. It is radio. You are right. It is taking the form of radio but solid."

Stella maneuvers the *Nautilus* down toward Europa. The sound becomes lower and sweeter as they approach the moon.

"Does the government know? I mean The Gutenberg, the Byron chain organization? Can they hear this? Can Ada?" Tinia looks wildly back at the satellite as it sparkles in space, getting smaller. "The government is behind this, right?"

"I think not," Stella replies, as she dives. She sinks them into the solid rock of Europa as if it was empty space.

"Possibly a new form of existence and certainly the end of life as we know it, but, no, this is not the government. No one knows what this is — yet," she says, driving them down into the center of the Jovian moon with her mind.

The Light Dark Sea

As Stella and Tinia sink, the moon around them decoheres. The sound apparently emanating from Europa becomes more melodic as they go farther down. They look for obstacles in their flight path as the sound gets louder. The moon transmits through solid stone. They make out songs which give back onto the simple sferics that first attracted Stella. These elaborate themselves further into admonitions and newsy bits. There are plain statements that on second thought seem not to be so plain.

"Things exist beneath the surface," Stella murmurs, drawing them farther away from the library, deeper into the moon.

"But why…," Tinia begins.

"Why go into it?" Stella says, as they go. "Don't you want to know? Don't you want to hear the cries, witness the music, this new…whatever it is? This sound. We've gone this far. When is it time to stop going? What don't we want to know?"

"But why me…," Tinia tries again.

"Why you?" Stella is supernaturally persuasive in this hypertransparent mode. She seems more of a traveler even than Tinia, in whose life there has rarely been a stationary moment. Stella is radiant with going.

"Because you are more congruent than I am with the pattern of being and moving here."

Stella takes hold of Tinia's arm, pushing her back against the paper deck of the *Nautilus*. Their faces are close. They smell each other's thoughtful sweat. Stella smells of tea. Tinia of sex. Tinia is distracted by Stella, very conscious of their straining, of what she perceives to be their closely matched strength. As always Tinia finds herself taking on the pattern of what is around her. The lines on her arms are like those on her face, making her the unwilling chameleon of thought and time travel, as if the very waves of space were imprinted on her skin. Stella is smooth and clear by comparison. The two women don't move at all and then they move, but not apart.

"You are young and scarred and scared. Sacred," Stella goes on, continuing to hold Tinia against the bulkhead. "Doesn't it feel…." She wants to say "holy?" but can't say it. "I can get us in," Stella says, letting go and backing off a little. "But I won't…I might not be able to get us out. Back. If, in fact, we can get back."

"Fuck." Tinia pulls away. "I was afraid of that."

She rests her head in her hands, collaborating with Stella's thinking. They think themselves farther into the moon and Tinia gives into the despair she has felt before every battle.

"People want to travel but they have no idea how much trouble it is," she thinks, using this and other thoughts to take them further and further down.

"It's just a big melodrama with them," Stella claims as they sink. Tinia knows she refers to the I. "It takes a person, a human, to cut through the crap, so to speak."

They burrow rapidly. Tinia feels all the space inside of her taken up by space. Something like liquid, viscous space or earth, like dirt but wet like mud, appears and coheres around them. Mud. Tinia feels muddled. She feels double scheduled or double entered, as if she were not the entering one. She finds herself counting backward and forward at the same time. A trick she learned on Mars. They drift as they dive. They seem to die.

"Tinia!" Stella says though she doesn't exactly say it. The moon sound has become deafening. Tinia is aware of something calling, crawling around inside of her. The inside seems to give way to what is further inside and so they go in together. They go down.

"Down," Stella comments as they traverse a void between densities. The rock is not so much rock as a collapsing of opportunities to be in space, to have space to move around in. Tinia feels the claustrophobia she associates with imminent exploding death. The next moment they hit the inner mud of the Europan being. Dark thoughts close around them. The stone closes. There is a lack of sky.

"Hold on!" Stella screams as they pass through a barrier of nothing into nothing. Beyond the barrier there is a violet light. There is a purple horizon on all sides. "Sky again," Tinia says, though she knows it isn't sky. She thinks of Ada's eyes, wondering idly why she can breathe here, why they are still alive.

"But why could I ever breathe," she thinks falling back again on war logic. "Why did I ever survive?" She begins to feel sleepy again, drifting into a reminiscence of the no-heart therapy she had after her escape from Mars.

"Now what?" she addresses the question to Stella, adding, as if waking up to it again, "Why have you brought me here?"

"On the contrary it is you who have gotten us this far," Stella closes in on her once more.

"She is like tea," Tinia thinks, longing for a cigarette.

"It is you who forget to die, Tinia. It is a thing you have, that and the caffeine or whatever it is. The tea makes it worse — or better. You are always slightly in retrospect. The rocks and mud. The war. And then we are here again."

Tinia looks into herself, as if to find these qualities but sees only stone. She becomes newly aware of the paper hull of the *Nautilus*, finding that they are, it is, caught in something. There is tearing and adhesion. Wrinkling. The *Nautilus* is floating or flying or sinking, depending on one's interpretation of this strange medium.

"Is this land?" Tinia looks around them.

"We are landing, or stopping, if that's what you mean," Stella says. She appears to have more density than usual, as if her translucence has hardened into gold. The *Nautilus* unfolds out of a solid wall into a chamber, a hollow.

"It's a cavern," Stella says. She realizes they are at the edge of something stained and yellow like a bruise and yet red, like blood. "Is it ocean?" she wonders looking down, finding it changes in response to her view.

"Them," she thinks automatically.

"YOU," the ocean says, cresting and seething, rearranging itself as if in response to a wind, though it is almost or even actually airless here and completely still. Tinia watches as golden tears roll down Stella's face.

The sea changes. It forms and breaks through a crust as of light on its surface. The surface in turn bends and collapses onto itself. The pattern is unmistakably like the swirling lines that appear lividly on Tinia. Tinia hold her arms out, blending into her environment. She sees herself like a fingerprint among fingerprints, as an ancient text or textile, as the whorls of a rose.

"*WE.*" The sea speaks again, causing Tinia's heart to seize up and her breath to be released all at once from her body. Tinia reaches for Stella, who crouches now, nearby, and finds that Stella is reaching for her.

Neither of them can move and then they both find a way to move toward each other. They wind their hands together, both grateful for the human touch in all this mud and stone. Tinia is livid with the pattern. It spreads through everything, energizing her, not unlike caffeine, she realizes dizzily, only more so. The edge of panic she also feels is, she decides, familiar and not entirely unpleasant. "Jesus," she thinks, "it's like a planetary rush."

The rocks whirl around them like weather. The sea is brittle. It is crimson. It breaks and seems to bleed.

"What is it?" Tinia says. "Or better, what is it not?"

"It's like the inside of space. Or they are. They are space but they are in not out," Stella replies.

"So are they alive?" Tinia asks, realizing it is beside the point, that everything is alive at least in the local sense and that the issue is more one of thought than life, if there is a difference — thought and talk. Talk and distance. She thinks of the I and sees a single I in her mind and then more I. And then, in living hideous color, she seems to see all the I at once.

"YES," they say and Tinia notes that they seem broadcast but corporeal, a dense idea of flesh like a tidal wave of being. The sea sings and mews. The sound sounds as if it were coming from mammalian nursery, a chorus, a zoo. There are roars and statements as if it were the I there heaving and roiling, for it is surely them, the women think, cohering among themselves, combining, recombining into a vast invasion like the one they thought they had left behind them, back in the universe.

Tinia and Stella look away from the sea and into themselves. They feel overwhelmed by consciousness as if they were on Earth but it is louder and hotter and more urgent and at the same time less, not exactly like a wound but like a very serious itch one needs to scratch. The women close in on each other.

Stella moans and they intertwine as if in conscious imitation of the recombinant I. They clutch at each other in a concentrated series of physical suppositions. They lay back into a cradle of stone, just up from the mud, overlooking the strange observant ocean. They fall, warm and dry, into their corner, permeable only to themselves, audible, pliable, while the bluish mud sparkles darkly below.

Stella, golden, shimmers against the green iridescence of Tinia, finding an opening in the scarred leather that covers her like skin. Tinia tears at the transparent things covering Stella, parting the layers only to find further layers, until Stella is apparently naked though, in a phenomenon familiar to her lovers, she seems more covered the more she opens herself. Tinia is patterned and there is a pattern on the pattern traced by Stella down into her. Tinia tries to speak or cry but Stella swallows each of her words until they are laughing and gulping breathlessly and Tinia sees Stella shed more golden tears.

"We need to explore this moon," Stella says, leaning, however, over Tinia on all fours like an animal in a cage.

"Yes, we have to plot the patterns," Tinia responds breathlessly, winding herself up around Stella.

Stella finds that kissing makes it hard to think clearly or easier, she can't tell, but feels that more kissing is called for to figure it out. Tinia concurs. They argue without speaking. They agree in silence, the moon humming, the ocean murmuring around them.

"What is it with them," Tinia finally says, looking out at the ocean. "They like to watch?"

"I think I'm in love," Stella says pulling her down.

"Shut up," this sweetly. They are tangled again, edging into the mud which has become a sort of golden blue. Bits of it cling, gilding them. They are illuminated by the mud, violet from above, red from below. Finally they break apart or open like the two halves of a mollusk, standing nakedly on the shore. They commence to wander as if they were not caught inside an alien moon on the edge of the solar system.

"Wait!" Tinia says when Stella reaches for her again. "Let's fuck without touching. Let's try it."

"I get you." Stella concentrates on Tinia. She realizes that the ecstatic quality of the stone and the sea and the melodic patterns there will continue to satisfy, distract, feed, and keep them afloat or alive or whatever it is they are, even if they don't touch. Something like communication seems to be occurring but is so persuasive, so exactly neutral to the mind and the skin as to be precongruent to one's feelings or decisions. So instead of sex their attention begins to adhere to an intricate exchange about the nature of the place. Or perhaps it is the same thing.

"I think I can read it," Tinia whispers or possibly thinks. They each stare at the other to see if they are speaking.

"IT CAN BITE LATE THEY TAKE," the sea says.

"They are not the only ones," Tinia observes.

"Quiet!" Stella says, listening.

They hear as well as see the patterns as if the whole ocean around them is a language they are newly able to use and which reflects something back at them with their own words, or at least their own letters, emphatically capitalized. It seems to be answering their unasked questions in a series of mirrored commentaries, exclamations and narratives that recombine like sex without necessarily being sexual.

"Though not necessarily not," Tinia thinks, zipping herself back into the outfit, brushing off a few flakes of shadowy blue mud and dust.

"Who are you?" Stella asks the ocean, feeling irrationally emboldened by recent events.

"TAKE NIGHT LOW," they begin, "US," they continue, "I" they add.

"That doesn't help," Tinia frowns, opening up also, even, if possible, more fearlessly than Stella.

And then she sees it. They both see *Ultravioleta* on the horizon, so close they feel they could touch the ship or that it could crash into them, and yet also far off and ghostly, like a bad transmission. They see Pontius enormous, horrible, both on the deck and bursting from the cabin. They see him fly from the mast like a shroud. They see Wyatt then, fading, lovely in his black and white, silken, silly, full of an inner wind that comes out of him like a dream of speech or like the silver saber they notice he has drawn. He and Pontius follow like paper dolls, linking arms, tearing away at each other, slicing through the ship and themselves, getting up, falling down, getting up again.

Wyatt spreads himself out on the huge mast like a sail or a sign. Pontius leers below in infinite duplication or perhaps their view of him is blurred. *Ultravioleta* goes in and out of consciousness and time. The ship is like a broadcast of itself, a projection of the past and future inappropriately combined, stuck together with paste and atoms, the patterns of which are peeled away in paper sheets, caught and torn on the stony ocean.

"LAY BY SLOW," the sea says.

"I can't know this," Tinia says, realizing where this is going. She sees familiar death like that in battle, constituting itself, the relentless destructive conflict of I with I, tearing at the tiny fragile world that surrounds them. "Time to go," she says, moving toward Stella.

But Stella lies semi-prone, feeling herself to understand the universe in new ways as projection and broadcast — a lovely feedback loop that repeats itself infinitely, as the rain of mere history wears everything down. Things become transparent, like herself, and constitute a particular delight. Stella can see it. The sea sings to her in something like I and there is a melody so invariant it can barely be thought of as song.

"Song," Stella thinks or sings, perceiving she is humming but not in her throat and not of her own accord. The sound seems to be playing her.

"Okay, yes, sing along, fine. But we have to go." Tinia reaches for Stella, half pushing and carrying her, she finds no tension, no usual pushing back. Stella is pliant with music, drunk with sex and thought travel. Tinia feels it too but is stiff with resistance. She leads as they make their way into the folds of the *Nautilus*. *Ultravioleta* looms behind them. The ship seems to grow larger and larger like a projected image whose light source is receding backward into space and time.

"Time to go to, baby," Tinia says, dragging Stella into the ship as the *Nautilus* closes and lifts.

"Time to have gone," Stella mutters sleepily as they begin to make their way back up through the mud and stone.

"You are not helping," Tinia whispers, after what seems like an eternity, though they have gone less than a stanza by any measure.

"Space is strange now," Stella comments as if they were already there.

"This is not space. This is rock," Tinia complains. "Try to focus. Not rock but rocket. Hello? Are you reading me? Stella! Try to have an inner life," she advises, slightly desperate. "Thought travel though rock," she thinks darkly. "It's a guaranteed headache."

Applying another strategy, Tinia forms herself into an arrow of time.

"Never fail to bring them back alive. That's me," she thinks. "Except for the times I died," she goes on, rising sharply as the rock demineralizes around them.

"YET DIE." She seems to hear a refrain from far below. "NOT."

Sensing a continuation of oceanic thought, Tinia continues to go up through the stone, feeling supported by the alien ocean, feeling, as always with Tinia and any medium, congruent, feeling, in the moment of thought, home.

"I," Stella wakes again, "go on." She is almost unconscious.

"You do go on," Tinia crumbles tea into a piece of paper ripped form the ship, lights it one-handed and exhales a fragrant cloud as she attempts to drive them up and out of Europa. But as they are about to break out of the moon they are reflected back down. Believing they are caught in another time storm, Tinia works frantically to bring them up, but she can't get them out.

"Oh no," Tinia thinks as they sink. "Oh goody," Stella murmurs like a sleepy child as they reenter the violet environs of the roseate Europan ocean.

Last Dance

Stella and Tinia recoil with horror as they see Pontius emerge from *Ultravioleta*. The great ship creaks and drifts in the stony sea in which they find themselves again. They hold their breaths as he speaks.

"The next bite is always the best bite," they hear Pontius comment to Wyatt. He speaks as if picking up an interrupted conversation. "Consuming is like breathing," he goes on. "First is last. Last always precedes the next bite or site, the next territory or terror. The next night. It's a great plan."

Pontius looks out. He seems to include the entire solar system in his hunger. He faces thoughtfully into Wyatt like a ship into the wind. They stand together on the paper decks of *Ultravioleta*, deep inside the Jovian moon. The Light Dark Sea opens before them like a map of itself.

Pontius' unrelieved sense of predation colors Wyatt's view into the center of the moon. Wyatt registers the unlikely and unwelcome presence of his erstwhile daughter-in-law and the mother of his son. These fragile humans appear small and needy.

"So be it," he thinks. "A person could solve a lot of personal and family problems looking at them from the Roman point of view," he says aloud, looking down at the glassy beach where the women seem simultaneously to be frozen in place and to run from him, from them. "Of course we are not really Romans," he addresses Pontius now, "or people."

"But we are," Pontius pursues. "From the governmental perspective we are people — citizens — Romans, if you will, our humanity, or inhumanity, is beside the point. That's the beautiful thing about the government."

"That it is complicit with the destruction of the people?" Wyatt asks.

"Only in the normal course of events," Pontius smiles.

Pontius looms out from *Ultravioleta* like a gas giant staining the sky, though the sky here is made of stone.

"In that sense they are only projections of themselves," Pontius goes on. "If we weren't almost entirely mental beings we couldn't eat them in the semi-non-corporeal form in which they exist in the universe. You know that."

"But we are and they do," Wyatt says.

"All the more reason," Pontius reasons. "They are not dead yet," he points out, "though the concept...."

"You are right, P, it interests me also, this death."

They have moved to a cabin in the ship whose paper, edged in gold, curls and seems to burn from the heat of their exchange. Pontius looms filling every corner of the space, outraging the apparent boundaries of his human form as well as those of the ship. To Wyatt he looks like money spilling out of an overstuffed envelope. A bribe to the universe already known to be no better than it should be.

"I am not long for this world," Wyatt says anticipating Pontius' next move.

"Right. But not just you, though, of course, you must die," Pontius agrees, surrounding Wyatt, as if it were an everyday event for an I to cease to be.

"All of them or at least most of them must be dealt with — the humans, the resistant ones, the robots, the ones that wander. This universe is not big enough for all of us," he smiles to himself, "like this ship and you and me. You and I."

Wyatt wonders what it will be like to die, realizing that it is unknowable by definition, he sees also that the man, the name, he occupies knows about it. They all know. And there is something else. Wyatt finds Ada in his mind. Her bright eyes question and advise him.

"Don't die," she says, "unless it is for them."

"Them?" he looks for a division among entities that would make sense of that distinction. He finds it easily enough in Pontius' hungry eyes. "Are we not also them then?"

"Where to die is to end," she thinks with him, "we are an other than result."

"So I die for them. Are they you? Are you Pontius? Am I?"

"Yes. For the humans," she says in his mind. "Or just for those you can see. But not for me. Not since I...not anymore."

"But Pontius…"

"…also dies," she continues. "In this version you die of each other. It's father for son, knight for knight — day for night — citizen for government, in the good sense."

"Pontius is the government? There is a good sense?"

"Not exactly, but in a way, yes. Not universal but more like a local good."

"I like it," Wyatt says, not liking it at all, but perceiving his death to be inevitable or at least symmetrical. "He doesn't know?"

"Oh he knows he is the government and he knows that I can die," Ada begins.

"And he knows that I can," Wyatt finishes, "but not that he can die."

"No, he doesn't know that. No I can imagine his own death or that you could cause them to die, us to die," Ada corrects herself. "Among the I, you are the only limit, the only contradiction."

Abrupt and brutal, Pontius bursts between them, obliterating Wyatt's connection with Ada, willing him into the continuum of the story he began with Marty on *Ultravioleta*. This story is a voyage, a deed, a scene, a duel, a deal.

"Let's go," Pontius says, as if to himself, blending Wyatt's face with his own, hungrily, brashly malevolent.

"Yes, let's," Wyatt turns away with deceptive mildness. He burns easily through Pontius' trick and through the confines of the ship he now thinks of as the imperial vessel of Pontius' relentless predation. He realizes that *Ultravioleta* is the con Pontius is running though he knows it is also the exquisite structure dreamed by Martinez. The very intricacy and resilience of the design allows for the epistolary quality of the ship to be turned into a weapon. The ship is the hidden message, the fragment of half-remembered song that turns out to be a dirge, this ship of fools or of state to be the Stygian raft, the barrel over the falls that are falling now.

Wyatt and Pontius parley. They waltz. They hide and they meet. They don't breathe so much as seethe together in sheer mutual resistance, Pontius to being taken and Wyatt equally to being eaten alive.

"I have been where you have lived most fully and taken what of you was yours," Pontius claims, streaming with mental sweat, heaving with malevolence.

Wyatt reacts by surging toward Pontius, tearing through the paper masts of the ship as it courses through the molten sea of the rocky moon, tearing them further down as he closes in on his killer, his twin.

"If you are speaking of Stella, it is hard to know how you can claim to steal what is by its nature, her nature, free." Wyatt speaks lightly, but he feels dark.

"The stolen thing is sweeter," Pontius says, his lips pulled back from his teeth in a bright smile.

Arms tangled like pythons, their faces plastered into the pliant paper of the vessel, Pontius and Wyatt burn through the ship and are reflected in the sharp glassy angles of the sea. Wyatt reaches a bit further out with his mind, trying to include everything, touching the minds of Stella and Tinia in their stunned animal stillness. Pontius revels in this display, looming, diving, driving them into and over the sea. He twists away and yet surrounds Wyatt, backing him down, keeping his prey always in sight.

In the distance are the women. They wake and walk and wander, hiding from view. Their unwilling reappearance has left them mentally exposed. They feel themselves to be nearing a catastrophic failure to avoid closure. They cling to each other like children being read the end of a fearful story. They flee. The sea beyond them on the bright beach crests and peaks sizzling in yellow and bloody crimson. The sunless sky is a purple desert in which *Ultravioleta* shimmers like a mirage.

"This sea is the source of everything," Wyatt realizes, with strange inner quiet, as he and Pontius reel wildly around the ship and around the inside of this tiny world, each attempting to stop, distract or assassinate the other.

"This sea," he goes on, "thinks. It thinks of me as existing in multiples. It is multiple. It — they — transfers the mineralized air into ideas, creatures. They are us," he realizes. "We are its beasts, the ones it dreams. We are the beasts of the sea."

"But we are not me," Pontius interrupts, closing in again. "I am I," he asserts.

Wyatt draws a mental sword, turning on Pontius in a menacing display of hyperconscious ego overblown even for an I. "I will see you die," he whispers.

Pontius is all smiles. To him the idea that Wyatt's death is worth dying for is axiomatic. Pontius' will is to stretch out the time of this hostility as much as possible. More than he wants to win, he wants to fight. He is the perfect opponent — quick, complicit, vindictive, evil, cheerful and vicious. Wyatt bows to his greater will with a greater willingness to die. He stretches further, faster, and farther out with the determination of the already gone. They work together to retain their point of contact, exchanging mental blows, sword to shoulder, sword to neck, decapitation just another in the series of endless, mutual gestures of brutality. Wyatt worries Pontius like a wind or a dog, trying to wear him down, wear him out. But Pontius grows larger with each blow. Around them *Ultravioleta* tears and burns, dipping beneath the red waves, piercing and pierced by the sharp angles of the Europan ocean. The ship fades in and out, foundering finally on the glassy shore of the Light Dark Sea.

Pontius and Wyatt are losing their concentration, becoming unconscious of thought and time, unaware of space. They are not unmindful of the hazards of their situation, but irresistibly they have fallen through time, fallen in love with death, with the inevitable outcome of their situation.

"WHY NOT STOP?" the sea says to neither or to both. The women scream, running, looking back, unable to bear this horrible repetition.

"Why indeed?" Wyatt closes in on Pontius on the beach, landing the fatal stroke between the little oceans of Pontius' eyes. At the last moment Pontius tries to turn away. He raises his vast empty hands into the violet air. He laughs and cajoles with his mind. His mental body writhes. He whines. He reaches into Wyatt, pulling out his heart and they fall together, arms out wide. Wyatt is still beating Pontius as they fall. His actions become those of a dead man. Pontius dies complexly, life after life draining out of him. Wyatt simply dies. Time crystallizes. The destroyed mast of the ship is wrecked and torn around them. The sails are no longer legible. *Ultravioleta* goes down for the last time.

The women have gone. Tinia sees Wyatt beat the lives out of Pontius, as they both seem to dissolve, spreading out against the airless sky. She and Stella leave it all behind. Tinia sees Wyatt die. Once more, she wills herself and Stella into the tiny shell of the *Nautilus*. She drives them up and out. Out and gone.

The Light Dark Sea seems to reverberate into the future, back into the past and then shimmers into the present again, heaving as the cosmos goes in and out of focus. The minds of all of the inhabitants of the universe are suddenly blank and then they are filled with an oceanic knowledge that bursts upon and among them like a solar flare. Of projection. Of the source of the I. Of the absence of themselves and the others. Of personal destiny and end things. There is an end to sleepiness and a desire to get back to something. Maybe it's work. These thoughts radiate out to all travelers marooned in space and time, telling them to stop, moving them on.

Second Sight

"I saw them," Cap says in answer to a question he is receiving, apparently from the government – or is the question coming from the people? He knows only that he doesn't care. Having entered into an observational mode pure even for a mechanic, Cap records. Record for record's sake, as he often says.

"I saw them go down. Yes. The ship and the men or the monsters. Whatever they are, were. They are gone now."

Back in the library, Dayv and the women lay dreaming in a heap. Cap tries to find Ada driving them around and around the moon as usual and then remembers it can't be Ada. He sees that Dayv is doing the driving, as well as the dreaming and the recording. He drives while he dreams and broadcasts while he dreams and he sleeps. Tinia dreams. Stella sleeps very deeply. Cap trails behind their thoughts, listening and primping. He watches their vivid sleep, more lively than other people's lives. Tinia's thoughts are particularly strong. She dreams hard, broadcasting brightly, tangled in the arms of her lovers.

"Humans are such sluts," Cap observes to himself, flying, hovering, recording. His spidery arms remake his face in a style redolent at first of the dark iridescence of Tinia and then edging into Stella's classic blondness. For Cap, history is more about style than events. The events are always the same. Monsters, death, apparent rescue, trust betrayed. In that way, the universe is like Mars and, like the café society of Mars, is a good place to put oneself on display, a good place to check out the accoutrements of the locals, their sense of proportion and limits.

"Idle thoughts of a mechanical day," Cap muses, drifting in orbit.

Making the record of the dreams of Dayv and the women is second nature to Cap, who is anxious to return to the inner part of the system now that things out here seem to be, as he would say, winding down. He feels the impatience of others to know what will happen with no I around — or are they really gone? His own disposition is entirely not to care, to record but not to notice.

"How can they be dead if they can't die?" Cap poses the question uppermost in everyone's mind.

"Where have they gone and will they be back?" he hears himself ask, also automatically.

"Oh, please," he thinks inwardly. "What could it possibly matter? People are so eager to be fooled."

Cap begins to receive a transmission from Robinson. There are multiple origins to the message. Cap guesses that Robinson has decohered again or at least become seriously blurred as a result of losing M. Something comes in about Mars, but Cap can't quite make it out. He reflects on the absurdity of a human and an I being partners and arrives at the conclusion that Robinson knows both too much and not enough. "A classic case," he decides, beginning to sense around him the consciousnesses of other stunned humans.

Tinia and Stella dream the loneliness of humans without their invaders. Dayv enables lazily, anomalously, seeming himself, as partly I, to be a remnant of what are now the old days. The universe is quiet and simultaneous. Where clouds exist, they are dark and roiling. Where curtains exist they are still but in tatters, shredded by the cosmic winds of recent events.

Eddie tunes in with his particular Martian doubt, looking for the break in the logic that will signal the complicity of the government — the incidental world-destroying blowback of any pseudo-historical events perpetrated by the malevolent entity he has come to fear even more than the I, more than the monsters of Mars. He sees it everywhere. He also sees Wyatt in the minds of the women, even before they have become aware of Wyatt's alien presence in their mental space. Nahid watches her lover watch the women and their dreams as they methodically relive the trauma of recent events. She writes everything down.

Tinia and Stella continue to dream together. Dayv dreams with them. They feel they have in common a searching, a groping for something, someone. Cap now realizes with a start that it is Wyatt.

"But how can that be?" he objects to himself.

Dayv and the women search for Wyatt in time configured as dreamscape. He appears to them suddenly, emerging from what seems like a cave. He moves first away and then toward them, stepping into existence as if their dream was a door, a corridor between universes. Wyatt and Dayv and the women think together about obliteration. Is it the same as death?

"It is the same," Wyatt says. "Give or take. I mean, it's eternal but it's also, you know, that day."

Wyatt faces fully into Dayv and the women, filling their sense of their capacity, filling also the metal mind of Cap, until they all make a single visage that seems to regard itself.

"Whoa, Nellie," Cap thinks. "You'd think the boys were back."

"Give or take a universe," Wyatt goes on. "We are gone."

"You have misplaced the universe?" Stella falls into the tenor of their old conversation.

"Yes, baby, but not yours," Wyatt replies smiling, as starkly black and white as ever.

"Not dead yet?" Tinia tries.

"But not alive." Wyatt dies again into their dreams of him. Something already dark gets darker as he disappears into it.

"Has he really died again?" Stella asks, but they can't tell. Finally, desperately, she breaks away, waking and rising, entering her ship, taking off. She leaves Tinia in a dreamless sleep on the deck of The Gutenberg, breaking from her thoughts of Dayv, from the absence of Ada, Stella heads out and away.

"Wait!" Dayv tries to say but finds she is already out of range.

Cap watches as they struggle mentally, dreamily, with the absence of the I and with each other. Dayv and Tinia seem not to have moved. Stella is by now a tiny dot in the distance. Wyatt has gone again the way of the other monsters.

"How many times is this guy going to die?" Cap thinks. "The problem was never the I anyway. It was always the government."

"It's the same," rejoins Eddie, who has been monitoring both the events and the nonevents of this day of days. Nahid sighs.

"No it's not. We're not the government any more than you are. We are real," Wyatt insists, but he is just an echo of himself, like an old song. "We are real," he repeats, "but we are radio — corporeal but on the air, of the air, like a program that is over. We are over. Over."

"It is a kind of death, being off," Cap reflects, but he has also already turned away. He feels the orbit of The Gutenberg decay infinitesimally behind him as he rises into space. Flying off, Cap wonders if the time of the paper ships has ended, but finds he doesn't know or, at least, that it doesn't matter.

"Where will they go if not to the library?" he thinks as he flies.

Again Cap receives a message from Robinson. This time it is a rather strident narrowcast. He thinks he hears the word "reruns." It is not clear what reruns could be but they sound grim. M is involved. Cap can't figure out where Robinson is going with this. He resolves to stop on Mars to find out and then thinks better of it.

Cap continues to record as Europa shrinks behind him. He turns toward the sun, recording the past with the mask in the back of his head. The library becomes a golden freckle on the outer edge of a pale moon. Cap himself doesn't look back. He makes his way away, partly in Stella's wake, partly in the familiar gravity of little Sol, so small in the distance. Arms akimbo, all of his faces facing out, Cap heads home.

Mother Sun

"Hello, Mama," Stella narrowcasts to Ada from the *Nautilus*. "I'm back." Stella should know that Ada is gone, but her mistrust of time makes her hope to find her lover at her usual station.

"Hello, Mama yourself," Dayv replies on Ada's frequency. "It has been my experience that you are never not away." What might be a complaint from anyone else sounds more like an invitation coming from Dayv.

"I'm turned around now," Stella says, recognizing Dayv's voice. She feels suddenly less sure of herself than she has ever felt. She wonders what one says to a son. Does one advise him?

"Why are you alive?" she asks, without thinking how this might sound.

"Good question, Mom. Why is any of us here? How do we survive? I don't know. I know that what is gone from me is enlivened by what is left. My ability to feel anguish is greater. I miss him. I miss them. I miss them all, especially Wyatt, but not only him. I started missing him well before he died. But like anyone, my life seems normal to me. I love the library. Ada made the difference. She was as great a teacher as she was a beauty – as you know."

Stella is reminded of her own endless grief. To her the universe seems made of sorrow.

"Can you talk me down?" she asks.

"I can talk you anywhere you want to go," Dayv offers.

"Home," she says. "What if I want to go home?"

"You've got me there."

They achieve the landing of the *Nautilus* onto The Gutenberg more with intimacy than drama. It is an unusual method for Stella who, except for her landings with Ada, has always depended on her own strength of mind to maneuver her craft. Soon she and Dayv are sitting together over tea in the library. Theirs is a strange continuum of human warmth and alien cool. Stella regards the creature who is her son. She wonders if she should hug him. Decides against it.

"This mingling of atoms," she thinks, very conscious of their proximity. "It seems like enough for now."

"Is enough," Dayv thinks back, pouring the tea.

"To absent lovers," Stella says, holding out her translucent cup.

"And to mothers," Dayv adds, bringing his cup to hers.

They sit in companionable hyper-caffeination, eyes closed, in the fragrant atmosphere of the tea.

"All my friends were monsters," Stella says finally.

"Friends and family," Dayv reminds her. "All monsters. All gone now."

They are silent again.

"I heard from Eddie," Dayv tries.

"And?"

"He writes but he doesn't really talk. He tries to talk to me, but I can't make out what he is saying. I think he's holding back. He doesn't trust me. It must be the Ada thing. It's not like he didn't know – shouldn't have known. There was a lot of anger in his last travel document. A treatise on Martian poetics. Its contradictions alone would be good for a pot or more — if you could follow them."

"It's a messy subject," Stella says, closing her eyes again, picturing the red world and its endless poets. "You've got the café people like Eddy and then, what do you call them, the systems? The people from the systems. I don't see how anyone ever gets anywhere with the stuff they write. It's always the same as something. What is the point of being the same?"

"People either get here or they don't," Dayv replies. "I never worry about the quality of the work. If it doesn't hold up they'll find out soon enough. It's their problem."

"I hate Mars." Stella stares straight ahead. Dayv is able to translate the remark.

"Eddie will be glad to see you," he says.

"The humans," Stella responds. "We're all that's left. Me, Eddie,

Tinia and a lot of Martians I can't relate to."

"Tinia," Dayv says fondly.

"You and Tinia?" Stella asks.

"You and Tinia?" Dayv counters. Stella looks away.

"No. I mean yes. Things were complicated on that trip to Europa. We were so far inside our own minds, not to mention the moon and the mud...."

"Yeah, that blue mud. She looks good in it."

"Tinia always looks good. But that was then – you know?" Stella peers at Dayv, trying to read him.

"I know," he says simply. He seems as calm as ever, even happy, and there is something else about him that Stella can't quite place and then she sees it. It is how he is toward herself. Even sitting, he towers over her with his elongated alien stature, but he also seems small and cuddly.

"This is my kid," she thinks, exploring unknown territory in her mind. She remembers the Stellar Display Ada had Dayv prepare for her. The personal universe evoked in this display, with its references to Mars, Wyatt and library science, suddenly seems to Stella more meaningful even than it was at the time.

"Did you like it?" Dayv asks directly into her head, seeing the reflection of the Stellar Display there.

"It was lovely," she replies feelingly. "I think it showed a lot of talent actually. Maybe genius. And it was," she struggles for a word. "It was sweet."

"Like Tinia," he pursues.

"Well, maybe not that sweet. Have you heard from her?" Stella asks. Her eyes narrow. "Is she still here?"

"She is here, yes. We are working together. She made something for you. She wrote it. It's part of a group of things called 'After All.'"

He hands her a tiny square notebook which he begins to open like a flower, but Stella stops him.

"I don't want to read it yet," she says. Stella feels too moved to speak. She knows that Tinia's piece will make her want to travel. She feels flushed and becomes more transparent.

"Tinia's work is almost like I contact," she says. "Except that it's not," she goes on, appalled to be missing the danger.

"I've got to go," she says, beginning to fade.

Dayv considers his mother. His brief whispered laugh is like a cry. Stella remembers that the I rarely laughed. She realizes listening to Dayv that she feels bereft of the crazy laughter of the I. She feels glad she has Dayv, glad that he is left to her.

"I love my son," she thinks, but says again, "I hate Mars."

"Give Eddie my regards," Dayv replies, quiet now. He looks down at his tiny mother. They walk through the library together. He knows she is going.

"But I can't go back." Stella looks out into space. The *Nautilus* opens before her like a book. She begins to blur as she enters into the familiar construct of the ship. Stella and Dayv look fully into each other. She holds his eyes for a moment. The whole universe seems present.

"You will come and go," Dayv says.

"I will come and go," she responds, though he sees that she has opened Tinia's book and is already reading herself away.

Blues missed as good as gone I am
On paper	This
Distance	Stained
Not that	Kissing
That	Villain is
Also gone	I am
When	She that
Is missed	Is not
Me that	Busted is
Stunned	Saying

Baby stay home meaning I must go On

Atelos was founded in 1995 as a project of Hip's Road and is devoted to publishing, under the sign of poetry, writing that challenges conventional, limiting definitions of poetry.

All the works published as part of the Atelos project are commissioned specifically for it, and each is involved in some way with crossing traditional genre boundaries, including, for example, those that would separate theory from practice, poetry from prose, essay from drama, the visual image from the verbal, the literary from the non-literary, and so forth.

The Atelos project when complete will consist of 50 volumes.

The project directors and editors are Lyn Hejinian and Travis Ortiz.

Atelos (current volumes):

Distributed by:

Small Press Distribution
1341 Seventh Street
Berkeley, California
            94710-1403

Atelos
P O Box 5814
Berkeley, California
            94705-0814

to order from SPD call 510-524-1668 or toll-free 800-869-7553
fax orders to: 510-524-0852
order via e-mail at: orders@spdbooks.org
order online from: www.spdbooks.org

Ultravioleta
was printed in an edition of 700 copies
at Thomson-Shore, Inc.
Text design and typesetting by Lyn Hejinian
using the Adobe version of Garamond
Cover design by Ree Katrak / Great Bay Graphics.